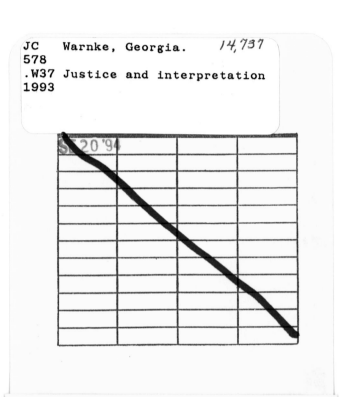

Justice and Interpretation

For Nathan, Alexander and Paul

Justice and Interpretation

Georgia Warnke

The MIT Press
Cambridge, Massachusetts

First MIT Press edition, 1993

Printed and bound in the United States of America.

Library of Congress Cataloging-in-Publication Data

Warnke, Georgia.
  Justice and interpretation / Georgia Warnke. — 1st MIT Press ed.
      p.   cm. — (Studies in contemporary German social thought)
  Includes bibliographical references and index.
  ISBN 0-262-23168-9
  1. Justice. I. Title. II. Series.
JC578.W37 1993
320'.01'1—dc20   92-34316
                                                                 CIP

CONTENTS

PREFACE

The presumption behind this book is that recent developments in political philosophy can be productively assessed under the idea of a hermeneutic or interpretive turn. By such a turn I mean that many important political theorists no longer try to justify principles of justice or norms of action on what might be called Kantian grounds: by appealing to formal reason, to the character of human action or to neutral procedures of rational choice. Rather, these philosophers suggest that if a society wants to justify its social and political principles it can do so simply by showing their suitability for it, that is, by showing that these principles express the meanings of the society's goods and practices, history and traditions. Thus, Michael Walzer appeals to the shared social understandings Americans possess of their goods in order to argue for principles of distributive justice that would represent what he calls a theory of complex equality. Alasdair MacIntyre emphasizes the different notions of both justice and practical rationality that issue from different historical traditions. And John Rawls now grounds his two principles of justice in a procedure of choice that is not supposed to be independent of the ideas or norms of any society but is rather to reflect an Anglo-American or Western understanding of the freedom and equality of moral persons. The common idea is that if we want to justify our political principles we must do so by showing simply that they are appropriate for us because of our history and traditions, our social practices and the kind of community we are.

Generally, the theorists I take to represent a hermeneutic turn do not themselves focus on the interpretive dimension of the above claim. They argue for the faithfulness and congruence of the principles they defend to the settled convictions (Rawls), social understandings (Walzer) and intersubjective meanings (Charles Taylor) of their society. But they do not consider the interpretive status of their view of what these settled convictions, social understandings, and intersubjective meanings are. They take themselves to be concerned with the meaning of our social goods, practices and traditions rather than with first principles of justice. But they do not explore the problems posed by the circumstance that meaning must always be understood and is often understood in different ways. This book is meant to fill this gap in the recent developments in political theory. It seeks both to exhibit the interpretive dimension common to the work of different authors and to explore the problems this interpretive turn raises. In particular, it will focus on the problems of conventionalism and subjectivism in that hermeneutic political philosophy seems to possess no standards for the adequacy of the interpretations it promotes. If we make the hermeneutic turn how are we to justify our interpretations of social meaning and how ought we to regard disagreements between equally well-justified interpretations? If we can legitimately disagree in our interpretations of our history and traditions, social practices and the kind of community we have become, of what importance is this interpretive conflict? Does it undermine the turn in political philosophy from the start or does it mean that the implications of this turn have not yet been fully drawn?

I shall be arguing that it means the latter and that to draw the implications of the interpretive turn more fully is to cast doubt on the idea of political consensus as the only ideal for us. Instead, just as we recognize that we can have different religious, moral and philosophical convictions in a pluralistic and democratic society, we must also recognize that we can have different legitimate interpretations of what the history, traditions, settled convictions, practices and, indeed, "conventions" of a pluralistic and democratic society mean. This conclusion raises problems of its own, of course.

ACKNOWLEDGEMENTS

Four institutions supported the research and writing of this book and I would like to thank them. The Bunting Institute of Radcliffe College offered me a Carnegie Non-Tenured Faculty Fellowship for the academic year 1986–87, during which time I was able to do some of the preliminary reading for the book. A Yale University Senior Faculty leave, a Summer Stipend from the National Endowment for the Humanities during the summer of 1990 and an invitation from the Institute for Advanced Study in Princeton for 1991–92 made it possible for me finally to finish the writing. Parts of chapters 1 and 6 appeared in *The Yale Journal of Criticism* and a version of chapter 2 appeared in *The Philosophical Forum*. They appear here by kind permission of both journals. For helpful comments on various versions of various chapters of this book, I would like to thank both the present and the former junior faculty in the Department of Philosophy at Yale, the Political Theory Group at Yale, the members of Kai Erikson's ISPS seminar at Yale, the Columbia University Seminar on Social and Political Thought and the Department of Philosophy at the University of California at Riverside. I am also grateful to Tom McCarthy, Ian Shapiro and Paul Stern for careful, if not always sympathetic, readings of the book, to my editor John Thompson for his support and to Pat Slatter for her skill and patience with a MacIntosh. Finally, I would like to express my appreciation to my four siblings, both for our general discussions over issues of justice and for their steadfast and unstinting support. If all happy families are alike, I am nonethless deeply grateful for them and for my husband and children, to whom this book is dedicated.

1

THE HERMENEUTIC TURN IN RECENT POLITICAL PHILOSOPHY

Jürgen Habermas has claimed four important features for a Kantian moral and political philosophy: First, such a philosophy is deontological in that it tries to justify norms of action and social practice in terms of rational principles rather than pregiven ends. Second, it is formalistic insofar as it does not proceed from substantive moral ideas, but looks, rather, for a neutral procedure for rational choice or moral agreement. Third, it is cognitivistic in that it tries to find a corollary for the truth of theoretical statements in the rightness of practical norms. Finally, it is universalistic insofar as its principles are meant to be generally valid rather than to reflect the intuitions of a particular culture or historical epoch.[1]

In contemporary Anglo-American political philosophy this Kantian approach has, perhaps, been most notably represented by John Rawls's *A Theory of Justice*.[2] In it, Rawls tries to provide a procedure for assessing principles of justice that will be both neutral with regard to different conceptions of the good and independent of the values and interests of particular groups or communities. In the "original position," individuals are to choose principles of justice from behind a "veil of ignorance" which is meant to deprive them of any form of knowledge that might prejudice their choice unfairly towards their own advantage. They are to be ignorant of their place in history and society, their race, sex or class, their wealth, natural assets and abilities and even of their values and conceptions of the good. These conditions are to assure that the choice of principles will be unbiased by a chooser's own situation and that the principles will be universal in scope, depending on no contingencies of time, place or socioeconomic position. Instead, they will be "the principles that free and rational persons concerned to further their own interests would accept in an initial position of equality as defining the fundamental terms of their association."[3]

At the same time, Rawls tries to correct the two-world consequences of Kant's own ethical theory by insisting that the choice of principles remains connected to empirical experience. Although parties to the original position choose principles of justice in ignorance of their particular circumstances and conceptions of the good, they do know that they desire certain "primary goods" that all individuals are said to want whatever else they want. Such goods include basic rights and liberties, opportunities and powers, wealth and income and the social bases of self-respect. Because choice in the original position is a choice of how these are to be distributed, the original position is supposed to remain both independent of individuals' specific desires and values while still intelligibly connected to human experience in general.

But some of Rawls's critics have argued that even a "thin theory of the good" such as this remains too abstract. Human beings, they argue, are motivated only by more robust theories of the good: by desires, values and purposes that tie them to cultural and ethnic identities, by norms of action that have developed in historical traditions and by ethical concepts that are bound up with one another in a rich, historically developed and, as it were, lived-in moral vocabulary. To deny the full moral weight of these identities, norms and vocabularies is either to condemn moral and political theory to irrelevance or to try to strip a community of the fullness and even richness of its existing ethical life.

In this book, I shall be concerned with the consequences of this sort of critique of Kantianism in political theory. Different theorists whose work I shall be exploring reject Kantianism to different degrees and in different ways, advocating various brands of communitarianism, neo-Aristotelianism, neo-Hegelianism and even liberalism. I shall be more interested, however, in what I take to be their common "hermeneutic" or interpretive dimension. My premise is that if we examine some of the different reactions to Kantianism in political theory in light of certain questions and issues that arise out of the German hermeneutic tradition, then we can both understand the insights that unite these different reactions and illuminate the problems they have not yet confronted. In this chapter, I shall briefly indicate the hermeneutic dimensions of two sources of dissatisfaction with Kantianism, then sketch the interpretive aspect common to some recent approaches to issues of justice and, finally, raise two problems with a hermeneutic approach so conceived.

The first source of dissatisfaction with Kantian approaches to political philosophy involves their abstract character. In searching for a neutral procedure for a rational choice of political principles, they seem to ignore the rich, lived-in character of the principles and practices a community may already possess. It may be, as Bruce Ackerman supposes, for example, that a group of travelers from different countries and different moral cultures meeting in some boundary context such as an uncolonized planet of our solar system would have to come to some agreement on principles of cooperation.[4] Furthermore, in order to do so, it may be that they would not be able to insist on their more robust conceptions of the good or on the rules of justice of their respective original cultures. In fact, it may be that they would be obliged to resort to some such neutralizing and universalizing device as either Rawls's veil of ignorance or Ackerman's benevolent policewoman who is to monitor any discussion of the principles for distributing the planet's or spaceship's goods.

Still, such circumstances might be said to reflect the exception rather than the rule, and even to be somewhat bizarre. Michael Walzer has suggested that the principles of justice or cooperation that would issue from either the veil of ignorance or neutral conversation would be principles only for some such multinational outer space delegation or, perhaps, for visitors to a hotel, visitors away from home and looking for temporary respite rather than the makings of a life.[5] Of course, some people prefer to live in hotels and others might want to begin a new culture with other foreigners on the moon. But the point here is that the principles upon which they agreed in order to do so would not necessarily have any relevance to the set of political norms appropriate "at home," for the culture they left behind. Every such culture is rather a historically constituted one, one that already possesses certain practices and that already takes certain principles, norms and values seriously. Political principles developed under universalizing conditions may be simply irrelevant to the concepts of justice that make sense to it because of the traditions of thought and action it already possesses. As Bernard Williams points out, the terms of a culture's moral and political vocabulary are "thick;" the vocabulary of the Anglo-American world includes terms such as *coward* and *lie*, for example; these terms are connected to the culture's practices and history and, more importantly, already provide its members with reasons for acting that are independent of the neutral procedures of justification to be gained by universalizing devices.[6] Williams insists, "A practice may be so directly related to our experience that the reason it provides will simply count as stronger than any reason that might be advanced for it."[7] That is, the practice on its own may simply be more compelling than the principles dictating its acceptance or rejection according to an artificial choice situation. As Walzer concludes in *Spheres of Justice*:

> Even if they are committed to impartiality, the question most likely to arise in the minds of the members of a political community is not, What would rational individuals choose under universalizing conditions of such-and-such a sort? But rather, What would individuals like us choose, who are situated as we are, who share a culture and are determined to go on sharing it?[8]

Kantian attempts to specify universal principles of justice give rise to a second dissatisfaction in addition to their disregard for the ongoing and lived-in character of a way of life. On the one hand, if we are to engage in a Kantian search for principles of justice to which "free and rational" persons in general can agree, then we have to guarantee somehow that those principles will be relevant to or be able to speak to the specific community for which they are intended, with all its historically developed concerns, values and purposes and with its thick moral vocabulary and political traditions. On the other hand, the very ideas and assumptions that condition the attempt to construct universally valid principles of morality or justice are themselves those of a historical community. We can insist, for example, that the principles of justice comply with the hypothetical choice of free and rational persons in an initial position of equality. Still, the ideas here of freedom, rationality and equality possess their meaning in connection with other meanings in our culture, with meanings to which they have come to be related such as those of human rights, fairness and entitlement, and meanings from which they have become importantly distinct such as exploitation, domination and hierarchy. The ideas with which we construct our ideal theories are thus already ideas which receive their definition within a particular context. They have developed over time, through the experiences of the culture and in association with the rest of its moral vocabulary. In this regard, they are entrenched in what the contemporary representative of the German hermeneutic tradition, Hans-Georg Gadamer, calls "effective-history" (*Wirkungsgeschichte*)[9] and related to one another in what Charles Taylor sees as a semantic space or set of meaning-constitutive distinctions and affinities.[10] It is not clear that they can be ripped out of this space or conceived of as free-floating and universally valid without also risking the loss of their own internal self-definition.

If a Kantian political theory suffers, then, from a neglect of both its own historical particularity and the rich moral life communities already inhabit, the focus of what I am calling hermeneutic political theory is precisely on the specific culture and set of historical traditions to which it belongs and from which its own "thick" vocabulary has developed. This political theory can be called hermeneutic, I think, because it takes a culture with its set of historical traditions, practices and norms as the analogue of a text. Its aim is no longer to construct procedures for an unconditioned choice of political principles. Instead, it attempts to uncover and articulate the principles already embedded in or implied by a community's practices, institutions and norms of action. The theory of justice becomes an attempt to understand what a society's actions, practices and norms mean, to elucidate for a culture what its shared understandings are so that it can agree on the principles of justice that make sense to and for it. As Walzer puts this point, "Justice and equality can conceivably be worked out as philosophical artifacts, but a just or an egalitarian society cannot be. If such a society isn't already here – hidden, as it were, in our concepts and categories – we will never know it concretely or realize it in fact."[11]

This kind of political theory claims that we neither need to nor can transcend our culture or history to find external grounds upon which to justify its political beliefs and practices. Instead, if we acknowledge both the thickness of our existing moral culture and the failure of attempts to find a neutral standpoint from which to assess it, then we ought not to worry about the neutrality or universalizability of our political beliefs and practices. Richard Rorty has suggested that we ought even to recognize that when we need rational justifications for these beliefs and practices we need them, not for just anyone, but for those with whom we are already involved and those who already understand the meaning of the moral vocabulary we use. Indeed, Rorty insists that we ought to be "frankly ethnocentric"[12] and admit that we accept the validity of our moral and political convictions for reasons peculiar to us, on grounds that make sense to us because of the history we happen to have had, but that may not make sense to others. Despite the criticism of his work, Rawls perhaps best sums up a similar position in a hermeneutically oriented restatement of his own approach: "What justifies a conception of justice is not its being true to an order antecedent to and given to us, but its congruence with our deeper understanding of ourselves and our aspirations and our realization that, given our history and the traditions embedded in our public life, it is the most reasonable doctrine for us."[13]

Two problems seem to arise immediately for a hermeneutic political philosophy, however. First, the focus of at least Rawls and Rorty on an internal justification of norms of action and principles of justice seems to indicate that a hermeneutic political philosophy gives up on the possibility of critical standards of justification. If we are simply now to show that a conception of justice coheres the shared understandings embedded in our public life, how can we ever question the institutions, practices, norms and actions that compose that life? How can we assess the rationality of our self-understanding? If one looks at the Hegelian origins of an interpretive approach, the depth of this first problem becomes clear.

Although the theorists I am calling hermeneutic do not explicitly ground their views on Hegel's work,[14] the two parts of their dissatisfaction with Kantian political theory — the emphasis on history and the stress on the lived-in or thick character of the moral world — can both trace their roots to Hegel's *Philosophy of Right*. In his preface, Hegel claims that philosophy's task is not to construct principles for a utopian society, but to try to understand the way we already live. "Philosophy," he writes, "is its own time apprehended in thoughts."[15] It cannot transcend its historical situation. Rather its task is to understand the rational core of the principles and practices we already possess, "to recognize reason as the rose in the cross of the present and therefore to enjoy the present."[16] Moreover, Hegel's conception of *Sittlichkeit* or the ethical life of a people is meant to point out the discrepancy between the abstract, ultimately empty principles of Kantian morality and the well-articulated moral world we already inhabit. Hegel's idea here, as that of Taylor and Williams, is that the meaning of moral concepts is constituted by their interrelations with others and that they develop these constitutive fields of contrast and affinity within the historical context of a particular community. Hence, moral deliberation cannot be understood against the background of the solitary, rational individual's principles, intentions or conscience; it refers us, instead, to the claims exercised within the institutional context of an ongoing form of life.

Both these ideas of historical particularity and *Sittlichkeit* are open to conventionalist readings, however. According to Joachim Ritter's influential studies of Hegel's political philosophy, the stress on historical context is not meant simply as an antidote to the excesses of ahistorical philosophical theory. For Hegel, philosophy's major problem was rather the challenge to historical continuity posed by the French Revolution and by the Enlightenment critique of tradition that it encouraged. The modern world sees itself both as having promoted reason over religion and custom and as having replaced servitude and hierarchy with the recognition of the principle of universal freedom. As Ritter reads him, Hegel does not want to retract this principle of freedom absolutely; however, he does claim that the stabilization of modernity requires that it be reconnected to the substance of tradition. To say that "philosophy is its own time apprehended in thoughts" is not to say simply that philosophy cannot transcend its own history; it is also to say that the task of philosophy is to relink its time to the past, to accomplish what Habermas in his account of Ritter's work calls a "historically enlightened traditionalism."[17]

Even if a hermeneutic political philosophy can reject this particular reading of Hegel's work, the traditionalism the reading promotes seems still to pose a problem. Hegel's reliance on the well-articulated ethical life we already possess had as an essential aspect of it the idea that this context was part of a logical historical development and that it already contained in embryo the principles that the rational state would fully realize. But suppose we give up the idea of this rational telos? Already in the nineteenth century, historians such as Ludwig von Ranke and Johann Gustav Droysen charged Hegel with not being historical enough, with basing the idea of a historically immanent rationality on a metaphysical conception of world-spirit's reconciliation with itself. Still, if we reject this metaphysical conception, how do we ground the rationality of the "concepts and categories" on which we focus our hermeneutic attention? If one gives up the idea of history's rational telos, all that seems to remain of the emphasis on historical context is a commitment to the present for its own sake, as the reflection of the experience accumulated in tradition. Tradition is no longer to be valued because it is immanently rational, because it is part of the path along which reason develops; instead, it is to be valued because, as Michael Oakeshott emphasizes, it is familiar: "Not *Verweile doch du bist so schön*, but, Stay with me because I am attached to you."[18] But if this kind of attachment is the consequence of moving from Kantianism to hermeneutics in political philosophy and if political philosophy must therefore give up its claims to be a critical enterprise, for many it will have also given up at least a large part of its own rationale.

In an essay entitled "Thugs and Theorists," Rorty expresses surprise at a remark Habermas makes in which he thanks German conservatives for their criticisms of him because they thereby assure him that he must be on the right track in trying to sustain a Kantian, universalistic approach to politics.[19] Rorty responds:

> I had taken it for granted ... that what made the right squeal was any *doubt* about ethical universalism, any suggestion of historicism, of the idea that there were no "universal and objective values" to be found in "human nature." Certainly most of the flak I have gotten from neo-conservatives has been centred on my scepticism about that idea. Such flak had helped convince me that *I* was on the right track.

Rorty attributes the difference here to the difference in the philosophical backgrounds of the German and the American political right. "Contemporary German apologists for Nazism ... often use an historicist philosophical rhetoric which talks a lot about "tradition," *phronesis*, and the spiritual situation of the age. By contrast, apologists for Reagan usually tell us that we need to recapture our sense of universal and objective moral values."[20] But whether or not Rorty is justified in his genealogies of German and American views, the question he has to answer is one Kantianism in political theory can avoid. How does one find a standpoint for criticizing one's culture and society once one gives up on "ethical universalism"?

One might argue that the problem for hermeneutics is still deeper. For the question is whether, in relying on the lived-in, thick character of the moral world, it is not relying on the ethos of a "folk" in a way that has already been shown to be a historical disaster. Certainly we might doubt the success of most attempts to prove the fascistic impulses behind Hegel's own work. Nevertheless, Herbert Schnädelbach, a critic of what he calls neo-Aristotelian approaches in political theory, claims that in stressing *Sittlichkeit* over *Moralität* these approaches leave no room for the autonomy of the individual. Moral principles cannot be grounded outside of the community. In fact, the idea of a *Letztbegründung* or ultimate foundation is not only impossible but immoral since it tries to go behind the institutional structure of a way of life; a principled morality can now be seen only as a private, fundamental opposition to the community itself and ethics and politics are reunited as simply the existing cultural ethos:

> If we remind ourselves of Kant, whose moral philosophy undertook to derive a categorical ought precisely under conditions of individual autonomy, then it becomes clear how dearly hermeneutics has to pay for its reduction of strong foundational claims. For Kant it was settled that autonomy and a categorical ought belong together and are not to be had independently of one another.[21]

Rorty raises a similar problem with regard to his own views. On the one hand he insists that we can assess our political beliefs only on a "frankly ethnocentric" basis, as those that make sense to us. On the other hand, as he succinctly asks, "What if 'we' is the Orwellian state?"[22] Even if one is less hysterical about the move from Kantian foundations in political theory to a focus on ethical life, the connection on which a hermeneutic political philosophy relies between justice and the interpretation of the meanings embedded in that life may be hard to fathom. If we cannot, in a sense, get behind the thick, historical meanings of a culture, how can we question their validity? And if we have to accept their validity as simply the lived-in quality they already possess, how do we avoid the conflation of ethics and ethos, or justice and tradition?

Rorty's reflections on Habermas's ethical universalism suggest the second problem that seems to arise for a hermeneutic political theory. If a hermeneutic emphasis on the meaning of a society's historical traditions and on the social understandings embedded in a way of life can be used both by conservatives against social democrats and by social democrats against conservatives, might this circumstance not indicate the subjective character of the entire hermeneutic enterprise? If political theory is now to be based on interpretations of meaning, will the theories and principles of justice it promotes not reflect simply either the talents or the obsessions of individual interpreters? Why should we accept either their interpretations or the conceptions of political life they base on them?

An example may help clarify these questions. Rawls now seems explicitly to base his two principles of justice not on an ahistorical, non-contingent procedure of choice but rather on a procedure of choice that is supposed to represent the meaning of our democratic political traditions. Thus the original position is now meant to model the freedom of democratic citizens in their capacities to choose according to what they take as their own rational advantage and it is meant to model the equality of citizens insofar as each chooses under identical conditions of ignorance. In *A Theory of Justice*, Rawls claims that the two principles of justice that issue from this modeling are first, that "each person is to have an equal right to the most extensive basic liberty compatible with a similar liberty for others"[23] and, second, that "social and economic inequalities are to be arranged so that they are both (a) to the greatest benefit of the least advantaged and (b) attached to offices and positions open to all under conditions of fair equality of opportunity."[24]

But surely we might understand our traditions of democratic citizenship differently: not in terms of an equal freedom to pursue our own advantage but, perhaps, in terms of either an equal protection of property rights or an equal participation in the political and ethical life of the community. We might therefore emphasize not the capacity "to form, to revise and rationally to pursue a conception of the good" as Rawls does but either the instrumental aims of society in protecting people's acquired goods or the capacity of citizens for shared deliberative activities. And we might require not that advantages to the most advantaged be balanced by some, however minimal, advantage to the least advantaged. We might insist that the advantaged deserve their greater share of social goods because of their greater contribution to their production. Or, alternatively, we might require that the least advantaged be guaranteed the economic, social and educational bases for active, deliberative participation in the cultural, social and political life of the community. How, then, can Rawls justify his principles of justice against either a more libertarian or a more republican conception of "the history and traditions embedded in our public life"? All three liberal, libertarian and republican conceptions would seem to require the reform of some of our institutions and practices. Hence, none of their conclusions can be viewed as issuing unproblematically from the meaning of our shared life as self-evident implications or uncontroversial notions of the meaning of our deep convictions and political traditions. But then how are they justified on hermeneutic premises at all? Might not different reforms be justified by different perspectives on the meaning of our public life?

I shall explore this sort of question more thoroughly both in the chapter devoted to Rawls's work and in the book as a whole. The two preliminary sets of questions I have raised in this chapter about a hermeneutic approach to issues of justice in general might be called those of subjectivism and conventionalism. They are interrelated. To take the problem of conventionalism first, the problem would seem to be that if no interpretation of our shared ethical life can show us why this form of life is a rational one or one worthy of our support, then the fact that we have different views of what it means seems almost irrelevant. Conversely, if we possess different interpretations of the meaning of our shared practices and norms and if we have no way of showing the superiority of one such interpretation to another, then it is becomes unclear what conventionalism can mean. Hermeneutic political theorists calling for the most substantial reforms in our practices and institutions as well as hermeneutic theorists content with the way things are will all be able to claim that they are being conventionalistic in that they are simply being faithful to the real meanings of these practices and institutions. But since this phenomenon will mean that a hermeneutic political theory can go either the way of "contemporary German apologists for Nazism" or the way of Rawlsian liberals, to mention only the two possibilities Rorty imagines, it might be asked whether a hermeneutic approach can help clarify issues of justice at all.

In the next three chapters I shall examine this question by exploring, first, Walzer's *Spheres of Justice*, second, Rawls's hermeneutic reformulation of the claims of *A Theory of Justice* and, third, the interpretive approach Ronald Dworkin presents in both *Law's Empire* and recent essays. I select these three versions of a hermeneutic approach because they seem to me to lie on both sides of the much discussed "liberal–communitarian" divide and, hence, seem to indicate the more fundamental character of the kind of interpretive issues with which I am concerned. In chapter 5 I shall examine Habermas's discourse ethics with a view to answering the question of whether the model of political decision-making it suggests can avoid these issues and in chapter 6 I look at the different ways Charles Taylor and Alasdair MacIntyre appear to confront the issues.

Despite the problems I shall be raising with regard to the work of all six theorists, I shall be also be using that work as well as the work of others to articulate in chapters 6, 7 and 8 a sort of solution to, or at least a way of rethinking the issues I have raised. This method might seem unduly cumbersome; it might seem that I ought simply to present the right way to think of potential conflicts in our social and political interpretations or, better yet, formulate the standards for picking between interpretations and showing the validity of one as opposed to all others. But I shall be arguing that there is no one "correct" or exhaustive view of a given society's shared meanings; nor is there a set of standards or procedures that could guarantee our agreement on one canonical interpretation of them. Just as we can have different understandings of a literary text, in a democratic society we can have different plausible and even workable interpretations of our own political traditions and social life.

Moreover, I shall be arguing that the consequence of this interpretive pluralism changes the task of political theory and that its focus should no longer involve adjudicating principles of justice but rather promoting discussion. The most important implication of a hermeneutic approach to issues of justice seems to me to be the centrality it requires of a notion of hermeneutic conversation. If a theory of justice is to be interpretive, it might also recognize both the partiality of the interpretations on which it is based and, therefore, the possible validity of alternative understandings of social meaning. Hence, political philosophy might look to the kind of debate and dialogue we find in the humanities as a model for the kind of testing, developing and strengthening of interpretations that might be appropriate to it. Not only political theory but politics might become dialogic in the sense that both would consciously pursue a kind of self-interpretive conversation in order to develop a more differentiated understanding of a particular society and hence a more grounded sense of which range of policies and practices are suitable for it. Politics and the political theory attached to it might be seen as forms of deliberative self-definition through which a democratic society develops itself. Sometimes that society may emphasize one self-interpretation or aspect of itself over another; sometimes it will backtrack in its policies and practices to pick up a lost strand of what it once took itself to be; and sometimes it may suffer periods of interpretive tension. Nonetheless, the task of both politics and political theory will be to foster a continuing conversation in which different possible self-understandings can find their voice. As we shall see, encouraging such conversation will also involve promoting the social and economic conditions that can make it fair and inclusive.

But if the task of political philosophy involves the promotion of a society's self-interpretive conversations, then the strategy I employ in this book of confronting a series of interlocutors is, however cumbersome, at least consistent with what I shall be arguing political interpretation, debate and decision-making themselves might involve. We shall need, I think, to find institutional ways of supporting a kind of hermeneutic public sphere in which different interpretive voices can be heard and attended to. We shall need to recognize that we can learn from each other and that our different senses of who we are can be reciprocally enriched by our interpretive conversations with one another. We cannot expect that all our conceptions of who we are as a society will always be reflected in our practices and political arrangements. Nor can we learn from everyone. Nonetheless, by pursuing the consequences of an interpretive turn, we can understand the way in which fair and equal hermeneutic discussion might supplement unanimity as a central political goal.

2

WALZER AND SOCIAL INTERPRETATION

In *Spheres of Justice*, Walzer offers an account of principles of distributive justice that is based upon an understanding of the meanings of different social goods. He argues that an examination of the understandings a political community has of its goods already itself indicates the principles according to which these goods ought to be distributed. This account of justice is explicitly pluralistic. Walzer argues both that different cultures have developed different distributive arrangements and that within cultures such arrangements can vary with the good to be distributed. Indian caste societies, for example, have traditionally adhered to a single distributive principle valid for all social goods and based on birth, while democratic societies, Walzer claims, have developed more complex criteria. Because of their social meaning, commodities must be distributed through the market, while, because of their different social meaning, offices must be distributed according to talent or qualification. Walzer denies that such variations in distributive rules — either within or among cultures — can be easily disputed. Rather, philosophical attempts to avoid pluralism, to unify distributive criteria according to the rules of an unsituated justice-in-itself, will necessarily fail. Not only do they disregard the different ways in which autonomous communities understand their goods; they also ignore both the internal distributive principles this understanding already entails and the internal autonomy of the different "spheres" of justice it can involve.

I start the present study with Walzer's work, because it exemplifies the kind of hermeneutic approach in which I am interested. Indeed, Walzer claims the Kantian approach of Rawls's *A Theory of*

Justice starts at too late a point. It tries to reconstruct the principles of justice rational individuals would choose under a "veil of ignorance" in which they were deprived of the kind of knowledge of themselves and their social and economic circumstances that would allow them to bargain for principles tailored to their own advantage. But in so doing, Rawls neglects the circumstance that before any good can be distributed, it must first be "conceived and created" as a good; moreover, goods are conceived and created in socially and historically specific ways. Whether and how education, property and political office, for example, are considered "goods" are questions differently decided by different societies and often decided differently at different points in their histories. Walzer concedes that "certain key goods have ... characteristic normative structures reiterated across the lines (but not all the lines) of time and space." Nevertheless, even reiterated goods are socially and historically constituted and although a good may be a good for many different societies it is not always a good in the same way. Bread, for instance, is variously conceived of as "the staff of life, the body of Christ, the symbol of the sabbath, the means of hospitality and so on."[1]

But if societies conceive of their goods in different ways, then the principles for distributing goods must be pluralistic as well. Bread cannot be available only on the market for those in a community who can afford if it is also, for that community, the body of Christ. Similarly, in a democratic society, education cannot be available only privately as long as it is crucial to full participation in the society. It might be available only privately if, as in ancient Athens, it is not tied to full participation. But for this very reason philosophical attempts to specify ideal conditions for choosing distributive principles for any society whatsoever will simply result in choices which are irrelevant to the ways historically situated human beings already understand their society and their goods. As Walzer puts the point, if we understand what a particular good is, "what it is for those for whom it is a good, we understand how, by whom, and for what reasons it ought to be distributed."[2]

This interpretive or hermeneutic approach to issues of distributive justice raises at least three questions that seem to me to go to the heart of a hermeneutic conception in general. First, what is the status of the social meanings that this account of distributive justice is meant to understand? Can different individuals within a community not have different ideas about their goods and, if so, what are the social meanings to which Walzer refers? Second, even if a theory of justice can rely on social meanings, how is it to justify its interpretations of them? Whereas Kantian political theory bases its conclusions on principles of rational choice or on the conditions of human action, Walzer offers only an account of meaning. But then why should we accept his understanding of this meaning? Are there not other interpretations of our shared social meanings that might be equally plausible? Finally, even if we were to accept Walzer's understanding, why should we necessarily also accept the principles of distributive justice that follow from it? If we substitute a hermeneutic or interpretive theory for a Kantian one, have we not precluded the possibility of taking a critical stance? As long as political theory is an interpretation of social meaning how can it avoid simply repeating the normative understanding a society already has of itself? I shall discuss each of these questions in turn.

Social Meanings

Walzer claims, "A society is just when its substantive life is lived in a certain way — that is, in a way faithful to the shared understandings of its members."[3] But do individual members of a given society always have shared understandings? And if they have some shared understandings can they not disagree in their understanding of other goods? Are disputes over distributive justice not a result precisely of such disagreements? Ronald Dworkin has suggested that Walzer's approach to issues of distributive justice is at least inapplicable to modern democratic societies since in these dissension and controversy are as pervasive as any common accord. As he continues: "If justice is only a matter of following shared understandings, then how can the parties be debating about justice where there is no shared understanding? What can it mean even to say that people disagree about social meanings? The fact of the disagreement shows that there is no shared social meaning to disagree about."[4]

Dworkin's objections have centered on Walzer's account of the meaning of medical care in the United States. On Walzer's view, this meaning is such as to place medical care within the sphere of needs. To claim that a particular good is a social need is to claim that the society considers it to be so important that it is necessary for all its members; moreover, it is to imply that no criterion other than that of need should qualify for determining its just distribution. One does not have to "stage a performance, or pass an exam, or win an election"[5] in order to acquire a social need; rather, those goods are identified as needs that members of a community consider essential and the provision of which serves as at least one basis for their establishing themselves and continuing as a community.

Walzer argues that the relationship between political community and the satisfaction of needs is reciprocal: Political communities form to satisfy the shared needs of their members and are sustained by the mutual indebtedness and solidarity that the provision of needs occasions.[6]

If medical care is commonly defined as a need, what are the distributive rules that can be derived from its meaning as a need? Walzer argues that if a community undertakes to provide some good to its members as a shared need, then it must provide the good to all of its members equally, at whatever level socially and technologically possible and in proportion only to their need. In other words, if a good is socially recognized to be a need, then the only criterion relevant to its allocation is that an individual or group needs it. Hence, considerations of wealth, birth or the like are external to the sphere of needs and their intrusion upon it constitutes an injustice.

This analysis of the logic of provision allows Walzer to criticize the distribution of medical care within the United States as just such an injustice. On the one hand, the United States uses some of its tax revenues to support medical research; it advocates general vaccination programs for the young, provides some care to the poor through the Medicaid program and underwrites an insurance system for the old in the form of Medicare. In Walzer's view, these arrangements point both to a social presumption that decent health care is a necessity and to a social commitment to providing it. On the other hand, it remains the case that Americans with money can buy better and more extensive care than those without. Middle- and upper-class citizens, Walzer says, are more likely to have a private physician, to visit him or her more often and less likely to be seriously ill than the poor. "Were medical care a luxury," he insists, "these discrepencies would not matter much; but as soon as medical care becomes a socially recognized need and as soon as the community invests in its provision, they matter a great deal."[7] On Walzer's view, there is no universal principle of justice that would require communities to consider medical care a need or to invest in its provision. It is not because the poor in the United States are sicker than the rich that the American distribution of health care is unjust. It is rather because the United States allocates some of its common resources towards the project of curing and preventing disease and in doing so facilitates cure and prevention mainly among the rich. This discrimination reflects a "double loss": Not only are the poor more ill, more often, they are also second-class citizens. "Doctors and hospitals," Walzer writes, "have become such massively important features of contemporary life that to be cut off from the help they provide is not only dangerous but degrading."[8]

But Dworkin argues that the issue of medical care offers little to justify Walzer's reliance on social meaning as a way of considering questions of justice. Certainly, the government's sponsorship of medical research as well as such programs as Medicaid and Medicare indicate some support for communally provided health care. But surely the very fact that Walzer criticizes — namely, that health care can also be privately purchased and is therefore unequally available to rich and poor — is also a fact that ought to count in reconstructing its social meaning. Why do these facts not show that Americans have different and even contradictory ideas about medical care? When they debate the issue of national health insurance are they not trying to determine just how medical care ought to be understood? How can Walzer assume that medical care already possesses a shared social meaning constituting it as part of the sphere of needs? Dworkin claims that even those Americans "who agree that some medical care must be provided for everyone, disagree about its limits."[9]

Put this way, this objection seems to miss the point of a hermeneutically oriented appeal to social meaning. To be sure, the ideas relevant to Walzer's own appeal are not ones he himself explores in much detail but they have been more exhaustively examined both in the hermeneutic tradition from F. D. E. Schleiermacher to Gadamer and in the so-called neo-Wittgensteinian philosophy of the social sciences. For both traditions the idea of social or intersubjective meaning follows from that of linguistic meaning. Indeed, the two domains of meaning cannot easily be separated. Words have the meanings they have in a language because of their relations to other words, because of their contrasts and affinities and because of the thick historical and social vocabulary they help to constitute and to which they belong. But they also have the meanings they have because of their relations to contexts of possible action and social practice. Hence the meaning of liberty in a Western democratic nation is tied to practices involving the freedom of contract and association, the possibility of voting and so on. At the same time, the meanings of these actions and practices themselves depend upon the availability of a certain vocabulary of concepts and ideas. That the activities of both voting and negotiating are the practices they are might be said to depend at least in part upon the contrast of these practices to a range of other practices such as bitter argument and deep consensus, the place of these activities within a field of norms and values such as tolerance and respect for others, and both their contribution to and dependence on a set of necessary conceptions such as individual self-reliance and free agency. The direction of dependence is not one-way. It is not simply because words such as tolerance, compromise and liberty have meanings for members of a democracy that they can participate in activities of negotiating and voting. Rather, it is also because of their participation in such practices and because such practices play the role they play in the society that the vocabulary of compromise, tolerance and liberty has the meaning and weight it has. Social meanings depend upon other social and linguistic meanings which in turn depend upon them and together these form a way of life.

It is striking that Dworkin does not seem to understand social meanings in this "constitutive" sense as part of a society's "thick" vocabulary and form of life. Rather, he treats social meanings as conventions or agreements between individuals *about* the social goods and social reality they share. Crucial to the concern with social meanings for the hermeneutic and neo-Wittgensteinian traditions is that such meanings are precisely not ideas about goods or about a given social reality; they are rather the meanings that constitute the goods as the particular goods they are and that constitute the interrelated elements of a given social reality as the form of life it is. The objections Dworkin raises to Walzer's use of social meanings seem more typically rooted in what Charles Taylor has called an atomistic social science.[10] The supposition here is that the meanings social goods, norms and practices possess simply reflect the individual opinions or ideas different individuals have of them. Individuals, in this view, develop various personal views about their activities, goods and institutions; they think of them in various ways and therefore disagree about how they should be distributed, and about how useful, moral and reliable different arrangements and practices with regard to social goods really are.

But such a conception of social meaning has been contested from Hegel on. Individuals are always members of societies before they start thinking about them and these societies already possess characteristic activities, practices, social goods and institutions. As members of societies and cultures, individuals possess a common language and common traditions, a set of practices that they understand and engage in together and a complex of commonly intelligible relations and modes of interaction. They also share a common set of goods that they all understand as goods. Hence, the personal views individuals develop with regard to their goods and social arrangements are opinions about goods and social arrangements that already have specific meanings. Social meaning is not a matter of the opinions individuals may have about goods, institutions and practices; it is a matter of the goods, institutions and practices themselves about which individuals have opinions.

Members of a given society may, of course, want its goods in varying degrees and engage in given practices to a greater or lesser extent. We may not all want money or power. Still, it is because we share an understanding of what these goods are that we can understand others who do want these goods in a society where these goods bring certain advantages with them, and that we can give an account of what would constitute their having acquired them. Taylor's own example of the meaning of the practice of negotiation is worth quoting at length:

> The actors may have all sorts of beliefs and attitudes which may be rightly thought of as their individual beliefs and attitudes, even if others share them; they may subscribe to certain policy goals or certain forms of theory about the polity, or feel resentment at certain things, and so on. They bring these with them into their negotiations, and strive to satisfy them. But what they do not bring into the negotiations is the set of ideas and norms constitutive of negotiation themselves. These must be the common property of the society before there can be any question of anyone entering into negotiation or not. Hence, they are not subjective meanings, the property of one or some individuals, but rather intersubjective meanings, meanings which are constitutive of the social matrix in which individuals find themselves and act.[11]

Clearly, Walzer cannot deny the existence of different opinions on the matter of a national health insurance for the United States. But it can be argued that these differences lie on a different level than that of social meaning; if Americans disagree on how best to provide medical care, they nonetheless share a rough understanding of what they count as medical care, what they count as physical health and longevity and how they understand their importance. Citizens of a country may not all want medical care to the same degree and they may disagree to what extent to provide it to those who do want and need it. Still, medical care has a common meaning for them and it is arguable that they can disagree so vehemently about it precisely because they all know, on some level, both what they are talking about and that they are talking about the same thing. Walzer's argument is that if Americans draw out the implications of this common meaning medical care has for them they shall also see that their disagreements have already been resolved and that they already agree on how health care should be distributed.

This analysis of social meaning does not settle all the issues Dworkin's objection raises. On the one hand, Dworkin seems to err when he suggests that differences of opinion about how and at

what level to distribute goods *already* indicate that no shared social meanings exist in these cases. On the other hand, he couples this criticism with a second objection that is not as easily dismissed. Even if it makes sense to conceive of goods as intersubjective or social meanings, it is not clear that Walzer has correctly articulated these meanings or, indeed, that they are always unambiguous or one-dimensional. Neither, therefore, is it clear that they are connected with a single set of distributive principles in each case. Walzer argues that the meaning health care has in modern industrialized nations requires that it be understood as a need. But insofar as he admits that the health care available to the rich is better than that available to the poor in the United States, it might seem that, according to his own analysis, a more differentiated understanding of its distributive mechanisms is appropriate for this society. In particular, it might seem that its American meaning is both that of a need and that of a commodity, and if this is the case it is unclear what methodological premises allow Walzer to emphasize such programs as Medicaid and Medicare while disregarding others in determining the meaning medical care has in the United States.

Although this question does not raise the issue of whether a hermeneutic approach to topics of justice can look to social meanings at all, it nonetheless poses the second question I raised at the start of this chapter — namely, how might a hermeneutic approach try to justify its interpretation of such meanings?

Social Interpretation

Even if we can allow that goods have intersubjective meanings how do we decide what the proper interpretation of a social meaning is? Does the history of health care permit us to pick Walzer's interpretation of it over a "mixed" interpretation emphasizing dimensions of both a need and a commodity? Depending on whether one emphasizes such programs as Medicare and Medicaid or the private distribution of care or both, it seems that one will be able to formulate quite different accounts of the social meaning at issue. As Dworkin puts this question:

> Shall we say that our traditions assign medicine to the market, with some inconsistent exceptions that should now be abandoned? Or that they assign medicine to the sphere of need but with inconsistent backsliding in favor of wealth and privilege? Or that they express the more complex principle that justice requires leaving medicine to the market but insists on just the qualifications and exceptions that we have

made? What could make one of these interpretations superior to the others?[12]

This question is one that both the hermeneutic and neo-Wittgensteinian traditions to which I have already referred have explored in some detail. The claim that literary hermeneutics has made from at least the time of Schleiermacher is that the adequacy of a given textual interpretation depends upon the extent to which it can show the text's coherence as a unified whole. Literary critics must reconcile all the different parts of a text — its chapters, for example, or the different lines of a poem — and show how these work together to compose a well-integrated meaning. Indeed, if certain parts of the text seem to contradict others, the initial presumption of the critic has to be that they do so because one or the other set has been misunderstood. The idea of a comprehensive unity of meaning guides the critical understanding and allows for a discrimination of better and worse interpretations of a text's various parts. Schleiermacher even argued that the meaning of any text had to be understood within the context of its author's life on the one hand and within the literary tradition to which it belonged on the other. It had to be conceived as one of the parts out of which the meaning of a life or literary tradition was to be constructed and hence had itself to be understood in terms of the life and literary tradition as a whole.

Of course, this conception of textual interpretation has more recently been criticized by a deconstructionist orientation. Deconstruction is not only indifferent but hostile to the notions both of integrated meanings and of contextual wholes. Instead, it claims, interpretation must search for the points of a text at which it undermines itself, at which its explicit intentions or meanings are betrayed by its own structure, syntax and vocabulary. Where hermeneutics stresses a holistic understanding that tries to provide for the point of each part of a text, deconstruction stresses disruption and the way in which the parts of a text work against each other and their author. From a hermeneutic perspective, however, even this approach must rely on a standard of coherence. Deconstruction must have an idea of what the intention or meaning is that is undermined by the text's language and structure and it must have acquired this idea from an appreciation of how various parts of the text at issue are meant or attempt to compose a unified whole. It follows that at least the initial aim of an interpretation must be to find the way in which the various sections, themes and arguments of a text cohere or are meant to cohere with one another to form an integrated whole and this point follows even if one's ultimate

aim is to show how the project fails. But this means that one interpretation is better than another precisely when it can find in the
text a more comprehensive coherence or even attempt at coherence that ultimately self-destructs. A hermeneutic approach, as we
shall see, need not claim that texts inevitably do form unified
wholes. At issue, nonetheless, are the principles necessary to understanding meaning so that interpreters can understand the problem a
particular text may have in articulating the unified meaning it attempts to express.

Following Schleiermacher, such theorists as Wilhelm Dilthey and
Gadamer claimed that the same conditions hold of both social and
historical understanding. The adequacy of an interpretation depends upon the extent to which it can make sense of a given
action or practice in terms of the larger context of which it is a
part; it depends, as well, on the extent to which it can show how
the understanding of the action or practice allows one to understand both other parts and the whole of which they are parts. Following Wittgenstein, such theorists as Peter Winch and Alasdair
MacIntyre made a similar point in criticizing positivistic approaches to the social sciences. The idea, they suggested, that human
behavior could be adequately explained by subsuming particular
behaviors under universal causal laws simply overlooked differences in the contexts of action available to different cultures. If we
are to understand historical actions or the practices of another culture we need to grasp them in light of the internally coherent form
of life they help constitute and hence proceed hermeneutically. If
we are to understand the activity of voting we must do so in light
of our understanding of the norms, history and values of the culture to which it belongs. Since we shall have to understand these,
in turn, in light of our account of practices such as voting, our
understanding will move in a circle. We shall start by understanding a particular action or practice in terms of our initial assumptions about the context of which it is a part, that is in terms of an
initial understanding of a framework of norms, values and activities. We shall then deepen or even revise that understanding of the
framework in terms of a more thorough understanding of each of
the parts that compose the framework, including the action or practice we initially tried to understand in terms of it. The goal is that
of ironing smooth all the wrinkles or glitches in our interpretation
so that we attain a self-consistent understanding in which our interpretation of the meaning of each practice, norm and arrangement of
the society confirms our understanding of the whole and in which
our understanding of the whole substantiates our understanding of
each part.

Walzer appears to follow similar hermeneutic principles in distinguishing "deep and inclusive accounts of our social life" from "shallow and partisan" ones.[13] His strategy is not to be caught by particular disputes such as those over national health insurance policies, but to move beyond them to understand the particular goods they involve within and as a contribution to the meaning of the wider context of norms, practices and institutions that give them their meaning. Hence, with regard to the issue of health care, Walzer does more than simply examine current health care distributions in the United States; he also offers both historical and sociological sketches of general transformations in the place of health care. He claims that the medical profession has always had a "bad conscience" about the link between health care and the market and notes that there have always been doctors who have accepted charity cases along with their paying patients. By the same token, the call of "Is there a doctor in the house" reflects a moral expectation that doctors will respond to emergencies without first investigating a victim's financial situation.

Walzer also contends that the Western conception of medical care has changed. Medieval Christians had little faith in the cure of the body and considered it legitimate that it was a luxury available only to the very rich because they also considered it largely superfluous. Concentrating, instead, on the cure of the soul, in which they had more faith, medieval Christians were concerned with easily accessible churches, regular services, the teaching of the catechism and so on. As confidence in the possibility of curing disease increased, however, and as that in the cure of the soul waned, physical health and longevity began to be taken more seriously. They began to reflect a "want so widely and deeply felt that it is not of this or that person alone, but of the community generally."[14] The idea developed that disease could be cured or prevented and, moreover, that since it could be, it ought to be. The licensing of physicians, establishment of state medical schools, public health campaigns and similar phenomena already signaled the growing commitment of the community to providing for the health of its members and this commitment was further developed through health education, compulsory vaccinations and the like.

This social and historical contextualization of current health care practices may provide some justification for Walzer's interpretation of their social meaning. It shows at least that the understanding of medical care as a need is not either superficial or arbitrary but rather reflects a deeper holistic interpretation. Nevertheless, the contextualization does not entirely resolve the issue we are considering. Even if one decides that a historical and social approach must be part of our interpretation of social meaning, one can still ask whether contrasting historical and social accounts are not possible. Why should we assume that Walzer's particular contextualization is the only proper one? Since he himself points to the medieval view according to which medical care was a luxury available only to the very rich, it might be thought that this view simply survives in the market dimension of current health care distributions.

On this interpretation, the present pattern of distribution reflects two competing traditions: a newer tradition of collective concern for the health of citizens and an older tradition for which health care is not yet a socially recognized need. To the extent that both traditions survive, a mixed interpretation of the meaning of American health care practices might be reasonably preferred to Walzer's own. Indeed such an interpretation might seem more complete than Walzer's since it tries to account for all of the society's health care practices without considering only some among them as representative of shared social meanings. On such a reading, American health care distributions reflect at least a two-dimensional meaning rather than a one-dimensional one, and the principles of distributive justice immanent to this meaning must therefore be similarly complex. As Dworkin writes, "We cannot just rule out, in advance, the possibility that though justice requires the state to intervene in the market for medicine in order to ensure that the poor have some care, it does not require that the poor be provided with the same medical care that the rich are able to buy."[15]

In this regard, Walzer and Dworkin appear simply each to present a different whole as the appropriate one within which to integrate the parts of the practice. Walzer concentrates on the historical context, on the historical tendencies suggested by the move away from conceiving of medical care as a luxury item for the rich only and towards a conceiving of it as a common need. In contrast, a mixed interpretation would focus on the diversity of the health care practices as they currently exist, suggesting that it is the present slice of life Americans share that must serve as the context for interpretation. But such differences in the whole that interpreters might take as the proper context for understanding meaning raise again the issue of whether a hermeneutic approach can really be transferred from the study of texts to that of social meaning. It seems not to be an issue for textual interpretation as to what the appropriate whole is within which the parts are to be reconciled. Texts have both beginnings and ends and these seem to demarcate the boundaries for any plausible interpretation of the text.

In contrast, in the sphere of social interpretation, we appear to be able to differ not only in how we understand specific meanings but

in what we understand the context to be to which they are supposed to belong as reconcilable parts. Neither the historical context
to which Walzer appeals nor the current practice criterion to which
a mixed interpretation might point seem to provide the set boundaries a text has just by virtue of being a text. History has no secure beginnings and ends as texts do. Instead, interpreters of
historical tendencies are always part of the history and on-going
society they are trying to understand. Whereas the end of a book
helps us understand which of its earlier parts are crucial, how they
fit into the text as a completed whole and so on, with regard to
social meanings we are always *in media res*. We do not know what
is going to happen in the future and, for this reason, we cannot
know what is important now. Are hospitals that operate for a pro-
fit, for example, the wave of the future or an isolated and temporary phenomenon? Are leaves for parents in the United States for
the care of infants or sick children in the process of becoming a
definitive element of American health care practices or not? Was
Thatcherism in England the wave of the future or a temporary real-
ignment of the society? A similar problem arises if we appeal to the
whole of present practice as the context of interpretation. Here, if
we are to agree in our interpretations of specific meanings, we
must also agree on what counts as the present. Does the meaning
of medical care in the United States include, for instance, changing
levels of support for certain aid programs, the shame many poorer
American citizens feel about receiving aid, or controversial practices such as state-subsidized abortion counseling? Again we seem
in media res and our interpretations seem tentative and unjustified
in a way that our literary interpretations are not.

But we are *in media res* with regard to literary interpretation as
well. One of the claims Schleiermacher made was that a text had itself to be understood within a whole larger than itself, a whole en-
compassing both the author's life and the literary genre to which
the text belongs. Hence, if the text constitutes the context for
understanding a part of it, it must itself be understood as part of a
larger context and its own beginning and end prove not to be the
proper context for interpretation. More recently, Gadamer has his-
toricized and radicalized this general claim. Both we and the texts
we are interpreting are part of history: we never understand a text
purely in its own terms as a self-contained and definitively bounded artifact. Instead, the way we understand a text is conditioned
by a tradition of interpretation, by the history of the text's influences on and relations with other texts, events and interpretations.
Even contemporary texts are part of a history of influences; not
only are their authors affected in various ways by various literary

traditions, but in interpreting them we are as well. We see them within a tradition of textual interpretation that already takes certain authors as classical, that has already developed certain standards of excellence, on the one hand, and of clichéd trivia, on the other, and that already recognizes certain literary styles and genres. Our interpretations are thus part of a history that has gone on before us.

They are, likewise, part of a history that continues beyond us. We can interpret a text in the best way that we know how. But we cannot know what new insights others will have into it after us, what new relations and connections the text will take on in the course of the history of its interpretation or what further interpretations our own interpretation may foster. The hermeneutic circle is a historical one in which we receive a text together with its historical context of influences (Gadamer's "effective-history" or *Wirkungsgeschichte*), interpret it from the vantage point of the influence on us, our concerns, preoccupations and the like, and then hand it down to the next generation for reinterpretation and assessment in line with their historical influences, experience and concerns. We are therefore never at the end of a text any more than we are at the end of history; in each case we remain in the middle with respect to meaning and our literary interpretations remain as tentative as our social ones.

These considerations mean that the problem of justifying an interpretation is similar for both literary and social or political hermeneutics. We can never have any understanding of a text or text-analogue that is not conditioned by our historical situation and by the constraint that being so situated in history imposes on our understanding of the proper contexts for interpretation. All our interpretations reflect the educated guesses of beings who cannot know how things will develop. The tendencies Walzer sees in the history of medical care may turn out to be a historical aberration in the long run. By the same token, the context that seems to justify a mixed interpretation of American health care practices may turn out to be simply a transitional step in a historical development that moves definitively away from defining health care as a commodity.

But, if all our interpretations must be tentative in this way, how are we to choose between them? Walzer himself claims that no understanding of meaning can be final and definitive.[16] But if this is the case, how can we justify our own particular interpretations against others? Since all are conditioned in one way or another and none can attain the "God's eye view" of the whole of history or of the best interpretive context, what criteria are we to use to determine the adequacy of our interpretations? Even if we can argue that the adequacy of either a social or a textual interpretation depends upon its ability to integrate whole and part, our position of ignorance with regard to the future makes it possible for us to take different wholes, and different possible histories, as the context into which the parts must be integrated. As a consequence, we may also develop different whole–part integrations and the initial question of this section returns at a deeper level: If the interpretation of meaning must be "deep and inclusive," how does one determine the correct boundaries for inclusiveness and hence choose between contrasting "deep and inclusive" accounts?

It is worth considering a familiar "intentionalist" response to this question since it makes a distinction between understanding and interpretation that we have thus far not made. The view E.D. Hirsch takes in his *Validity in Interpretation* is that the only possible standard for the adequacy of an account of textual meaning is its conformity to the intentions of the author of the text. Texts have what he calls "determinate meanings;" he implies that interpreters correctly understand those meanings only when they manage to work themselves out of the contingent historical meanings to which the text may have been related and correctly reconstruct the original meaning the author "willed" to convey or the author's "verbal meaning". While it is true, Hirsch concedes, that an author cannot will language to mean whatever he or she wants, it remains the case that the determinate meaning of a text is correlated not with accidental historical developments but with its author's intentions, provided that the linguistic system the author uses allows the words to have the meaning he or she wills for them. As Hirsch puts this claim, "Verbal meaning is whatever someone has willed to convey by a particular sequence of signs and which can be conveyed (shared) by means of these linguistic signs."[17]

Once interpreters have correctly reproduced the author's verbal meaning, Hirsch allows that they are free to relate that meaning to whatever contents they want or think will be relevant to their audience. On his account, this is, in fact, the role of interpretation as opposed to understanding; after interpreters have understood the meaning of a text as determined by the author's intentions they must explain that meaning to others and, if the text belongs to another age, this explication will often involve employing more familiar and meaningful terms or examples than those used in the text itself. But Hirsch insists that this circumstance "by no means implies that the meaning of the text varies from age to age or that anybody, who has done what is required to understand that meaning, understands a different meaning from his predecessors of an earlier age." Although Coleridge and George Kittredge may understand *Hamlet* differently, it does not make sense to say they understand it differently because they come to the text from different historical situations taking different historical wholes as appropriate contexts. Nor can they both be right about its meaning. There is only one verbal meaning and, therefore, only one valid understanding of the play, although there may be many good explanations or interpretations of its meaning that do vary with historical circumstances and the concerns of various audiences. Thus Hirsch concludes that any perplexity about *the* correct meaning of a text, a perplexity issuing from the different contexts in terms of which it can and probably has been interpreted, derives simply from a failure to distinguish understanding from interpretation. "The historicity of interpretation is quite distinct from the timelessness of understanding."[18]

Might we not, therefore, avoid the problem that we have just located in a hermeneutic approach to issues of justice by employing the intentionalist strategy Hirsch employs for texts? The correct understanding of a text, social practice or good will be that one which identifies the author's or agent's intentions, whereas differences in interpretation will be admissible as differences simply in views about the significance of the text, social practice or good or about the best way of explicating meaning to different audiences. Such an appeal to intentions is the strategy R. G. Collingwood does take up as the correct approach to the meaning of historical events and actions. If we are to arrive at an objective understanding of the battle of Trafalger, we must understand it the way it happened, or, in other words, the way Nelson understood it.[19] We must work our way back into Nelson's mindset to understand why he acted as he did and hence what the meaning of his actions was. But, even if this is the right route to historical understanding, it is not clear that it is open to the interpreter of shared social meanings. As we have seen, the meaning of social practices and goods cannot be reduced either to converging personal impressions about social phenomena or to collections of individual intentions because such impressions and collections of intentions are always about social practices, goods and institutions that already possess meanings. Social meaning is not a product of ideas in individuals' heads; it is a product, rather, of relations and contrasts to other meanings – to other practices and goods – about which individuals have ideas and intentions.

Moreover, even if it *were* possible to reduce social meanings to collections of individual intentions, an intentionalist account of social meaning would still have to indicate how we are to *understand* individual intentions. This problem obviously arises for historical and textual meaning as well. The question is how the meaning of an intention is any more self-evident than the meaning of a text – or of an action or practice. We still have to understand the intention as something[20] as the intention to convey one meaning or another. But how are we to verify that our understanding of the intention is correct? We can read the intention off the book, as it were, working back from the meaning we apprehend in the text to the intention we think the author must have had. Since we are reading the intention through our reading of the text, however, it is hard to see how the former can provide support for the latter. We might appeal to the author's letters, diaries or conversation to ground our understanding of his or her intention. But then we shall have to know how to integrate this sort of evidence with the text.

Rather than resolving the problem of understanding meaning, Hirsch's solution seems to move it back one step. We now simply have to understand the meaning the author willed to convey. But we shall still be involved in a hermeneutic circle of whole and part, one which now has the author's intention instead of the text as its object and we shall therefore still have to determine which evidence is relevant to the author's intentions, which intentions or aspects of those intentions are relevant to the text and how they can be integrated with one another into a coherent unity. If there is more than one way of doing this, if a given set of intentions may be understood under different interpretive contexts, as a part of different accounts of the author's life, for example, and if not only the relevance of a set of intentions to the text but the text itself can be understood differently, then the solution Hirsch proposes will simply reiterate the problem at hand: how do we decide which intentional evidence to include in our understanding of a text and how shall we understand this intentional evidence and its relation to the text?

As long as we take meanings as our object there seems no way out of the subjectivism of interpretation. If we try to resolve ambiguities in the meaning of a text by going beyond the text to the author's intentions or to psychological or historical facts about its author, we still have to figure out how best to understand the meaning of these facts and intentions. Similarly, if we try to resolve apparent ambiguities in the meaning of our notion of health care by looking at its social and historical context, we still have not only to determine the appropriate context, but to "read" this context in some way. In neither case is it clear that there will be an obvious and unique way of understanding the evidence to which we appeal or, indeed, that we will agree on which evidence is relevant. Dworkin may criticize Walzer's approach insofar as it takes

certain aspects of our ideas and practices to be more important than
others. Indeed, another critic has claimed that Walzer's claims are
simply "arbitrary and tendentious."[21] But were Dworkin explicitly
to propose a mixed interpretation of the meaning of medical care,
a "holistic" interpretation relying on the current existence of contradictory practices rather than on a historical dynamic, would this
proposal be any less interpretive or any less partial than Walzer's
own? The difference between a mixed interpretation of medical
care and Walzer's interpretation is that they take different practices,
events and historical changes to be significant, that they emphasize
different arrangements and relations and that they begin with different contexts as the whole into which the various parts on which
they focus are to be integrated. But both remain interpretations.
And the same would seem to hold of any attempt to adjudicate between them; it can itself appeal to no ultimate evidence or uninter-
preted, "brute data."[22] Rather, even the evidence to which we
might appeal to judge between two proposed interpretations must
itself be read and understood in some way or other and one critic
may read and understand this differently than another.

It is not clear then that we can retain Walzer's own distinction
between "deep and inclusive accounts of our social life," on the
one hand, and "shallow and partisan accounts," on the other. Two
different interpretations of either textual or social meaning might
be equally deep and inclusive; they might offer equally well-integrated accounts of the relation of part to whole; they might each
offer internally consistent interpretations of the text of our social
life that can each show how that text or life composes a unified
meaning. Still, these different interpretations will be also be equally
partisan; they will offer interpretations that are necessarily selective,
that emphasize different practices, norms of action and institutions
and that place these within different historical contexts and social
frames of reference. The same partisan character will hold of any
attempt to adjudicate between them.

To what Taylor calls "the authoritative conception of science in
our tradition" this ubiquity of interpretation is a scandal and the
same might be said for political theory. If there is no non-interpretive way of deciding between different possible interpretations of
social meaning, then it is not clear how a hermeneutic political
theory can defend a single or canonical set of distributive principles
for any particular good. The distribution of health care in the United States can rather be a just distribution in a number of ways, depending upon how one interprets its meaning. We can make
doctors complete civil servants, as Walzer suggests; we can make
them complete capitalists, as Robert Nozick suggests; or we can

even require them, as Dworkin might be taken to suggest, to be a mixture of both. One might claim that the conflict of interpretations presents no problems for literary hermeneutics since no grave consequences follow from the possible existence of different but equally deep and rich textual interpretations. Indeed, it could be argued that the existence of different interpretations is vital to the enterprise of literary hermeneutics and that, for the humanities as a whole, the entrenchment of single canonical interpretation of meaning would be devastating. But what of politics? Here, it seems, we cannot simply appreciate differences in interpretation; we need to determine a set of principles, to distribute goods in one way or another, and to decide controversial issues. The conclusion that no interpretations of meaning are any more definitive in this domain than in the humanities, would seem to indicate the limits of a hermeneutic approach to questions of justice. This conviction is perhaps only magnified when one considers how the problem of conventionalism emerges in Walzer's work.

Social Criticism

Suppose we do agree on a single interpretation of the meaning of a given social good or practice and suppose that we even agree on the larger social and historical context to which that meaning belongs. Another problem arises for a hermeneutic political theory: namely, that if we have no basis for defending our principles of justice other than that they issue from that which we agree are our shared social meanings, we seem to have no reason to defend rather than oppose them. Why, in fact, should we engage in the task Walzer sets himself of pushing shared social meanings to the immanent conclusions they possess for a society's principles of justice? To derive such principles from interpretations of shared social meanings seems to tie the principles to the ways in which a community already understands itself. But communities have obviously understood themselves in racist, sexist, fascist and otherwise objectionable ways. Hence binding principles of justice to social meanings seems to involve binding them to the ethos of a people in a way that can and, indeed, has been disastrous. Interpretation is imprisoned within the circle of a society's self-understanding and, because it is, it can never move from the interpretation of social meaning to a critique of the society that may be urgently required.

On Walzer's view, the connection between principles of justice and the shared understandings of a community does not preclude the possibility of what we might call external criticism. His example is that of traditional caste societies which distribute goods in radically unequal ways and justify this distribution on the basis of prerogatives of birth. The shared understandings of such societies may stress the individual's responsibility for his or her own fate and define the equality of human beings such that this equality is meant to span many lifetimes instead of one. If a person receives less of a certain good than another person, then this distribution may be justifiable from the perspective of the society itself on the basis of the caste system. The meaning may be not that a person or group is being discriminated against, but that that person or group must work to be more worthy in another life and merit a larger share.

It is surely not possible to criticize such a society's distribution of goods on the basis of its own shared social meanings. Nonetheless, Walzer insists that we can use our own political tradition to criticize the principles of justice that operate here and we can do so precisely because of the different shared understandings our tradition involves. In fact Walzer claims that the activity of Western visitors to a caste society who might try to argue its citizens out of their conception of their social goods is "entirely respectable."[23] The crucial point for Walzer is simply that such criticism issues from a particular culture and historical tradition and hence from a set of particular social understandings. There is no transcultural court of appeal or non-conventional account of a "justice in itself" rich enough to legitimate these beliefs against others or others against them. Both sets of principles flow from situated contexts, from the shared social understandings of a particular cultural group. Hence, the terms of the criticism we might make of caste societies are the "thick" ones to which Bernard Williams refers, ones historically developed in association with the other terms of the moral vocabularies of Western democracies and in the context of the West's general practices, social and cultural assumptions and distributive arrangements.

This account of social and political criticism leads to difficulties as it stands, however. For, if we criticize a society such as a traditional caste society for its treatment of the lower castes but also claim that our criticism flows only from our own social and political understandings, the criticism also seems to lose most of its force. Indeed, if we acknowledge that our notions of justice and equality are based simply on shared understandings that are peculiar to our culture or tradition, it is not clear why we should object to the different shared understandings of a different culture and tradition. Their version of the meaning of equality may not conform to our own. Nor, however, do we need to abide by its distributive consequences. More importantly, it is not clear why the members of the other society should object to what to us may be its inequalities. In trying to convince members of a caste society to change their social understandings, we can only be asking them to move from one "local account"[24] of equality to another and it might be understandably unclear to them why they ought to do so.

One of Walzer's responses to such relativistic quandaries is to point to the possibility of what he calls internal criticism. As long as external criticism remains external it has many of the same deficiencies as Kantian political theory. If one criticism of the principles that are meant to issue from a Kantian theory of justice is that they are disconnected from the rich ethical life that a community already has, principles issuing from the shared understandings of one culture and tradition may remain similarly disconnected from another. Internal criticism therefore tries to show how a community's own particular practices or distributive arrangements violate its own deep meanings or, in other words, how these practices and arrangements fail to keep faith with the shared understandings internal to the form of life itself. The hermeneutic circle we mentioned earlier is crucial here as well.

In interpreting a text, we project a unified meaning for the whole of the text on the basis of our understanding of some part or parts of it; we then use this understanding of the whole as a basis for interpreting other sections of the text and revise our interpretation of the whole if it cannot integrate the new meanings we have discovered. We may then have to return to our understanding of the initial parts of the text and revise it to cohere with the general meaning we are now projecting. But at some point, we may also simply have to abandon the hope for coherence and reject those parts of the text that are inconsistent with the most general meaning we can discover in it. The same can be said for social interpretation. At some point we may have to concede that certain actions or practices are simply inconsistent with the meaning our norms, institutions and public values compose as a whole. Internal critics therefore stress the actions, practices and understandings that seem to fail to form part of a coherent whole as they understand it and that deviate from the overall meaning a form of life seems to possess. Thus, Richard Rorty argues that the American involvement in Vietnam was not wrong because it violated some universally valid notions of freedom and national self-determination. It was wrong rather because it violated the shared social understandings of United States citizens themselves. As Rorty writes, the United States betrayed its own "hopes and interests and self-image."[25] Walzer's criticism of health care practices in the United States can be argued to work according to the same principles; it is supposed to show that these practices also betray our historical hopes and self-understanding. His most striking example of the way part and whole fail to cohere in the United States is suggested by his analysis of the Pullman case.

In 1880, George Pullman founded the town of Pullman in Illinois, a planned community for workers producing his Pullman coach, dining and parlor cars. The town had no municipal government but was instead owned and managed by Pullman in the same way he owned and managed his factories. The schools in the town were "at least nominally run by the school board of Hyde Park Township," but every other store and service from the gas stations to the fire department was owned and run by Pullman and his employees. More importantly, the town regulations were George Pullman regulations. Pullman decided how many churches the town could have, where liquor could be sold and even the proper attire for lounging on the porch of one's home. In 1898 the Illinois Supreme Court ruled that this kind of management of a town was "incompatible with the theory and spirit" of democratic institutions[26] and ordered the Pullman company to divest itself of all its non-factory property.

Walzer finds this decision contradictory. The thrust of the decision, he argues, is the claim that ownership of property in a democratic society does not entail political power and it does not entail political power because of the general meaning, "the theory and spirit," of our traditions, history and institutions. George Pullman could have owned all the houses and stores in Pullman, Illinois and, as his tenants, his factory workers could have also paid him rent. Still, it was thought to remain contradictory to the theory and spirit of democratic institutions that he should also control their lives and that the town should possess no means of democratic self-rule. But, Walzer argues, if the thrust of the decision requires keeping property ownership and political power separate within a town, then they ought to be kept separate within a factory as well. No more than the ownership of a town does the ownership of a factory and its machinery justify a dispensation with the principles of democracy. Hence, the theory and spirit of American institutions requires, in addition to political democracy, some form of industrial democracy and, in addition to political self-rule, some form of worker self-rule. As Walzer concludes:

> an economic enterprise seems very much like a town ... It is a place not of rest and intimacy but of cooperative action. It is a place not of withdrawal but of decision. If landlords possessing political power are

likely to be intrusive on families so owners possessing political power are likely to be coercive of individuals. Conceivably the first of these is worse than the second, but this comparison doesn't distinguish the two in any fundamental way; it merely grades them. Intrusiveness and coercion are alike made possible by a deeper reality – the usurpation of a common enterprise, the displacement of collective decision making by the power of property ... If this sort of thing is wrong for towns, then it is wrong for companies and factories, too.[27]

The principle of internal criticism that Walzer uses here to criticize the political prerogatives of factory ownership has affinities with the idea of immanent critique within the tradition of Western Marxism. The advance Marx thought he had made over moralistic attacks on capitalist society was that his critique was internal to bourgeois society itself. Immanent critique is meant to hold up bourgeois society's own norms and ideals to the society itself, to show the way in which capitalist economic practices necessarily undermine the principles of freedom and equality that are part of bourgeois society's own self-understanding. Hence, for Marx, because labor is bought and sold as a commodity on the market, the idea of freedom under capitalist conditions becomes a form of wage-slavery; equality becomes the dependence of one class on another and the right to property becomes the right of one class to appropriate the products of the labor of another.[28]

Walzer himself refers to both Marx and the Italian Marxists, Antonio Gramsci and Ignazio Silone, in defending his view of internal criticism. As Silone writes, social criticism starts

by taking seriously the principles taught us by our own educators and teachers. These principles are proclaimed to be the foundations of present-day society, but if one takes them seriously and uses them as a standard to test society as it is organized ... today, it becomes evident that there is a radical contradiction between the two. Our society in practice ignores these principles altogether ... But for us these are a serious and sacred thing ... The way society butchers them ... fills us with anger and indignation. That is how one becomes a revolutionary.[29]

But Marxist social criticism claims an objectivity that Walzer can no longer claim for internal criticism. In moving from the sphere of exchange to that of production, Marx claims to be achieving a true account of what is really going on in a capitalist economic system. To the extent that members of the society fail to see behind the ideology of freedom and equality to the real social conditions this ideology occludes, they remain bound up in a false consciousness.

Walzer doubts whether this kind of argument can be sustained. "Perhaps," he argues "the greater number of workers believe that the equality realized in capitalist society is genuine equality or that it is equality enough."[30] Hence their consciousness is not false; it is simply their consciousness.

The problem here is that one might say the same for democratic politics: namely, that for the majority of Americans, political participation outside the factory is self-rule enough. Hence, if Marxist ideas of objectivity and false consciousness have to be discarded it also becomes unclear why Walzer's own interpretation of the Pullman case should not be regarded with scepticism. Just as we might advance a more mixed interpretation of the meaning of medical care, we might also argue for a more differentiated concept of the relationship between property and political power immanent to American practices and institutions. Moreover, we might advance a different view of the coherence of this relationship with American traditions and self-understanding as a whole so that what appears from Walzer's perspective as a contradiction in the understanding of politics in town and factory might appear as entirely consistent with "the theory and spirit" of the relevant institutions.

The upshot of these considerations is that the problem of subjectivism that we raised for social interpretation also arises for social criticism. Internal criticism rests on an interpretation of the nexus of norms, ideals, practices and institutions in a society to which one or more particular actions, practices and institutions are said to fail to cohere. But if this form of criticism rests simply on interpretations or, more precisely, on an interpretation, first, of the meaning of the whole and on an interpretation, second, of the meaning of both the parts that do cohere and those that do not, then it may also reflect simply one perspective on this nexus. The role of the United States in Vietnam may contradict what, according to Rorty, are the hopes, interests and self-image of the country. There were certainly Americans, however, who thought their country's hopes, interests and self-image required its intervention. In general, a hermeneutic approach to social criticism seems necessarily to face the possibility of not only critical interpretations of a given society but equally plausible non-critical and even apologetic ones. All of these may be equally comprehensive; all may equally well integrate part and whole. Nevertheless, to every critical interpretation it may always be possible to contrast a non-critical interpretation and even a different critical one. Hence, to take an interpretive approach seems to risk making of our political theory a kind of Hamlet writ large. We shall have so many interpretive possibilities for understanding our history and tradition that we shall become equally paralyzed with regard to both thought and action.

Of course, it might be claimed that such a bewildering array of critical and non-critical perspectives on a given society would at least be less worrisome than one monolithic and thoroughly degraded interpretation. Thus, it might also be said that any society that must live with the problem of subjectivism, or with the problem of a conflict of interpretations, at least avoids the problem of conventionalism with which we began this section. For, if we have different understandings of what our traditions, practices and historical experiences mean, we might also have different ideas of what fidelity to our shared social meanings entails and, hence, different ideas of what being conventional involves. In my view, we must concede that Walzer's interpretations of social meanings are partisan interpretations. They seem to be best grasped as attempts to intervene in the self-understanding of the United States and to present it with a way of understanding itself that Walzer hopes will become conventional. If others argue with this interpretation, Walzer insists that he can only continue to offer it: "The critic can only speak again, more fully and more clearly."[31] Still, the idea of a plurality of such critics all speaking more fully and more clearly remains disheartening. To which of them should we listen? On what basis might we decide which interpretations are better and which worse? What context for interpretation ought we to select in a given case? In the next chapter I shall look at Rawls's attempt to cut through such an interpretive cacophony and to forge a consensus over that conception of justice which can win the support of what he terms an overlapping consensus.

3

RAWLS, PLURALISM AND PRAGMATIC HERMENEUTICS

Walzer's approach to questions of distributive justice relies on readings of the shared social meanings that are embedded in the traditions and practices of American society. This approach seems to have no way of justifying either its particular reading of these meanings or the principles of justice it infers from them. One might argue that a given interpretation of social meaning is justified when it is supported by the reading of other shared meanings in the society and, therefore, when the relevant range of shared social meanings coheres internally to form a unified whole. But different interpreters may disagree on what the relevant range or field of meaning is, how it does cohere internally and which whole the meanings are supposed to form. If we take as the relevant field of meanings those that emerge within a particular historical dynamic and if we emphasize the direction in this dynamic then we might consider Walzer's interpretation of the United States's medical care practices to be superior to a mixed interpretation. In contrast, if we take the totality of present health care practices in the United States as the relevant "whole" and if we grant equal significance to each action or event, then we might judge a mixed interpretation to be superior. But how can we determine which interpretation of the meaning of health care is better since any frame of reference we might employ to adjudicate between them will itself involve a decision about meaning? And if we cannot adjudicate between possible social interpretations how can the kind of internal social criticism to which Walzer points be compelling? This chapter will consider answers to these questions suggested by Rawls's recent work, since, as I remarked earlier, we might consider this work to be the clearest indication for a "hermeneutic turn" in political theory.

Rawls claims that his theory of justice remains Kantian in that it still seeks to establish a procedure through which rational agents are to specify principles of justice under reasonable and fair conditions. As he writes, "The leading idea is to establish a suitable connection between a particular conception of the person and first principles of justice by means of a procedure of construction."[1] Hence, parties to an "original position" are still to choose principles of justice behind a "veil of ignorance" and this veil of ignorance is still to prohibit them from tailoring principles to their own advantage by depriving them of the sort of knowledge that would be necessary for them to know what their advantage is. The theory is less Kantian, however, in that both the conception of the person and the connection established through the original position between it and first principles of justice now possess social and historical foundations. The principles of justice that are chosen in the original position are meant both to be ones for a specifically democratic regime and to correspond to the "deeper bases of agreement" embedded in its historical traditions.[2] Indeed, Rawls insists that this starting point leaves entirely open the question of whether these principles can also be extended as a general political conception to different societies existing under different historical and social conditions.

Thus, just as Walzer relies on shared social meanings, Rawls sees his task as that of articulating a conception of justice that conforms to the settled convictions and deep self-understanding of a constitutional democracy. For both Walzer and Rawls, the examination of questions of justice is an interpretive enterprise; the theory of justice is not meant to erect that "beyond, supposed to exist" which Hegel already criticized.[3] It is supposed, instead, to work out a conception of justice that issues from the traditions and social meanings already contained in a shared political culture. As Rawls writes,

> The aim of political philosophy, when it presents itself in the public culture of a democratic society, is to articulate and to make explicit those shared notions and principles thought to be already latent in common sense; or, as is often the case, if common sense is hesitant and uncertain and doesn't know what to think, to propose to it certain conceptions and principles congenial to its most essential convictions and historical traditions.[4]

If Rawls's theory of justice is thus hermeneutic in a sense similar to Walzer's, Rawls resolves the problem of justifying an interpretation by creating an implicitly pragmatic hermeneutics.[5] He begins where we ended our analysis of Walzer's approach to issues of justice; namely, with the situation of diversity and the question of consensus.

Pragmatic Hermeneutics

For Rawls, the necessity of what I am calling a hermeneutic approach to issues of justice stems from the "fact of pluralism" and what he calls the subjective circumstances of justice in modern democratic societies. Because of the Protestant Reformation, the wars of religion that followed it and the subsequent development of principles of toleration, modern democratic societies are characterized, according to Rawls, by a range of different moral, religious and philosophical doctrines as well as by different more specific ideas of the meaning, value and purpose of human life. The point of a conception of justice, however, is to provide the citizens of a democratic community with a set of common standards for adjudicating the legitimacy of their political institutions and practices, a set they can all accept and publicly acknowledge. Where there exists a diversity of comprehensive doctrines and of what Rawls calls conceptions of the good, any attempt to ground principles of justice on only one such doctrine or conception must make it unacceptable to citizens who adhere to or pursue another. If a conception of justice is to be generally accepted, then the principle of religious toleration must, Rawls argues, be extended to philosophy and morality themselves. A conception of justice for a pluralistic society must depend for its formulation and justification, not on particular moralities, religions or philosophies, but on the specifically political ideas and traditions of the society itself; as Rawls puts it, it must issue from the "intuitive ideas viewed as latent in the public political culture."[6]

Thus, the hermeneutic turn in political philosophy presents itself as simply the best alternative to basing principles of justice on comprehensive metaphysical, moral or religious doctrines. We must look to the meanings embedded in our public political cultures because to draw our conception of justice from any more general and comprehensive doctrine, including the comprehensive moral liberalisms of Kant and Mill, would be to be dogmatic. Since these moral liberalisms rely on substantive notions of the value of human life and on ideals of personal virtue, they seek to impose their own moral view. In Rawls's view, they are to be contrasted to a strictly political liberalism that is worked up solely from the store of fundamental political ideas a democratic culture has developed in the course of its history. Rawls insists that such a strictly political liberalism applies only to the basic structure of society or, in other words, to the framework of basic institutions and norms. Furthermore, it is meant to elaborate simply an appropriate conception of justice for these basic institutions where by appropriate is meant a conception that follows only from strictly political understandings democratic citizens can share in spite of substantive differences they may have with regard to philosophy, religion, morality and ideas of the good.

This description of Rawls's turn to a hermeneutics of our public political culture is incomplete as it stands, however. As members of a democratic culture our differences can extend beyond different ideas of the good and beyond different comprehensive religious, moral and philosophical doctrines to encompass different understandings of the meanings embedded in our shared political culture. On the one hand, Rawls introduces his conception of justice as a means of resolving the conflict in a democratic society over two possible interpretations of its history and political traditions.[7] The Lockean interpretation emphasizes the so-called liberties of the moderns – namely, the liberties of civic life such as freedom of thought and conscience as well as certain basic rights of the person, property and association – while the Rousseauian interpretation emphasizes the liberties of the ancients – namely, the equal political liberties and values of public life. On the other hand, however, Rawls often writes as if this conflict were a conflict simply over which principles of justice conform to fundamental intuitive ideas of the public political culture on which its members agree; at other points he claims it is a conflict over which institutional arrangements are necessary to realize the values inherent in that culture, "how the values of liberty and equality are best realized in the basic structure of society".[8] From these points of view, the task of a political philosophy is to formulate principles of justice that can resolve the conflict between Rousseauian and Lockean traditions by producing a public agreement merely on which institutions and practices accord with the meaning of the political history and with the common self-understanding of democratic societies.

The presumption here, then, is that this political history and self-understanding can be interpreted in only one way, at least within a given democratic society. The manner in which Rawls employs the idea of "reflective equilibrium" in his "Justice as Fairness: Political not Metaphysical" confirms this presumption. There he argues that a theory of justice begins by collecting certain firm convictions that the members of the society share; "the belief in religious toleration and the rejection of slavery" are the examples he gives. These provide "provisional fixed points which any conception of justice must account for if it is to be reasonable for us." In formulating a conception of justice we then "look ... to our public political culture itself, including its main institutions and the historical traditions of their interpretation, as the shared fund of implicitly recognized basic ideas and principles." The attempt of a theory of justice is to articulate this shared fund and to match it up with the settled convictions we have already fixed. Rawls concludes, "a political conception of justice, to be acceptable, must be in accordance with our considered convictions, at all levels of generality, on due reflection."[9]

But the "fact of pluralism" is not a fact just about the diversity of general moral, religious and philosophical doctrines in a modern democracy. Nor is it a fact just about the principles, institutional arrangements and practices that best realize the meaning of its public political culture. It is also a fact about our different understandings of the meaning of that public political culture itself, about the meaning, for instance, of such ideas and principles as freedom and equality. Indeed, even if we possess "a shared fund of implicitly recognized basic ideas and principles," we may nonetheless place different emphases on different aspects of this fund, understand the relation between these aspects in different ways, stress different dimensions internal to them or understand the fund itself within different contexts of interpretation. Where these circumstances hold we may come to understand the meaning of the fund differently as well.

The case of medical care in the United States served us in chapter 2 as an instance of this deeper hermeneutic problem. Where Rawls does recognize it, the conception of justice he presents has an additional practical orientation to that indicated above. Its task is not just to produce principles of justice that are reasonable or workable for us, given our shared understanding of the meaning of our public political culture. The idea must rather be to fashion the starting point for such a shared understanding. The conflict we must resolve is not simply that between Lockean and Rousseauian interpretations of the arrangements and principles of justice appropriate to us given our history and tradition. We have also to resolve the conflict between Lockean and Rousseauian interpretations of what our institutions and historical traditions themselves mean. When Rawls is clear on this task he claims we can accomplish it only by presenting their meaning *in a particular way*. As he writes, "If we are to succeed in finding a basis of public agreement we must find a new way of organizing familiar ideas and principles into a conception of political justice so that the claims in conflict, as previously understood, are seen in a different light."[10]

We can clarify this idea of the task of social interpretation by comparing it to Walzer's idea. If Walzer's own idea is that the point of an account of justice is to present an interpretation as clearly and as fully as possible and to present it even more clearly and fully if it does not win immediate support, Rawls's view of interpretation is pragmatic. He seems to admit, sometimes anyway, that we can have different ideas not only of which principles of justice we ought to establish but of what our shared institutions, understandings and traditions themselves mean. On this assumption the task of interpretation is not to present *the correct* picture of this public political culture but merely to present a plausible picture in the hope that the picture will be accepted. Much more often than Walzer, in fact, Rawls uses terms such as "acceptable," "workable," "suitable" and "congenial" when describing the grounds for his principles of justice. The point is not to get at the "real" meaning of our ideas and settled convictions. It is rather to provide the grounds for social agreement, by providing an interpretation of our ideas and settled convictions that we hope can be attractive to us all.

The role of a theory of justice is thus pragmatic in two senses. On the one hand, it is meant to provide a mechanism for producing a set of principles that are workable or practicable for members of a democratic regime and hence that produce agreement on its basic structure. It could appear that this set of principles can bring about an agreement on the basic structure of society because they reflect a deeper basis of agreement already existing in the political culture and tradition. On the other hand, however, the theory is meant to produce agreement just because it depicts the meaning of our shared political culture in a way that is workable for us, that we can all accept. Hence, Rawls's project is not simply that of understanding *the* shared meanings implicit in our institutions and practices and of formulating *the* principles that conform to those shared meanings. His considered view seems rather to be that in proposing principles of justice we must look to our public political culture because we cannot look to comprehensive doctrines and that we must propose a conception of justice that complies with a certain picture of this public political culture, a picture on which we can all agree even if it does not satisfy all of the intuitions and interpretations on which we differ. It would be too strong a claim to insist either that the conception of justice that emerges from this strategy is uniquely determined by our public political culture or that the understanding of that public political culture embodied in the picture we give of it is uniquely correct. We need to find a description of the meaning of our political ideas and traditions that is not as much faithful to those ideas and traditions in all their possible dimensions, as simply practicable for the project of securing agreement on principles of justice.

Thus, if we can understand Walzer's *Spheres of Justice* to offer an interpretation that Walzer thinks others should accept, we can understand Rawls as offering a conception of justice to the members of his democratic culture that he thinks they will find reasonable because it offers a workable interpretation of meaning on which they can agree. Rawls's recent accounts of both the function of the original position and the idea of an overlapping consensus help further to clarify such a pragmatic hermeneutics. They both also help to illuminate somewhat further the complexities of a hermeneutic approach to issues of justice.

The Original Position and the Idea of an Overlapping Consensus

There appear to be at least three ways of comprehending Rawls's notion of the original position. As he formulates the idea in *A Theory of Justice*, it might appear as if the original position were supposed to mark an "Archimedean point"[11] external to any existing society and therefore capable of assessing principles of justice on grounds independent of its own norms and standards, Rawls says that the original position represents the "philosophically most favored"[12] description of the initial situation in which parties form a "social contract" and he even describes it as part of rational choice theory. As noted earlier, parties are to decide on the terms of cooperation behind a veil of ignorance and hence without knowledge of their social and economic circumstances, of their race and sex, natural assets and abilities, historical situations, values, attachments and conceptions of the good. The principles of justice are those "that free and rational persons concerned to further their own interests would accept in this position of equality to settle the basic terms of their association."[13]

But the account of the original position in *A Theory of Justice* is open to another interpretation as well, an interpretation according to which Rawls is not concerned to use it to formulate the basis for a socially and historically unconditioned choice of principles of justice. Rather, it is meant "to account for our moral judgments" and to form part of a "theory of our moral sentiments."[14] In this formulation it remains unclear whether Rawls assumes a unique interpretation of a society's moral judgments and sentiments. Still, the function of the original position here is not so much to present a philosophically favored description of the initial situation in social contract theory as to offer a "device of representation," as Rawls calls it in his more recent work. In situating parties behind a veil of ignorance, the original position models those conditions of freedom and equality that, as members of a democratic society, we already think reasonable to impose on our representatives in their determination of principles of justice for us. That is, it represents in a particularly lucid form our intuitions with regard to both the freedom and the equality of democratic citizens in determining the design of basic institutions and distributive arrangements. The "reasonableness," here, of the design of the original position complements the "rationality" of the parties to it. They are to choose autonomously, in line with their interests, while the veil of ignorance assures that they choose in a way that accords with our basic moral intuitions of fairness and equality.

Rawls's reliance, here, on conceptions of freedom and equality remains problematic, however, as long as it ignores the problem of interpreting *these* conceptions. According to a third view of the function of the original position, it would have to serve not simply as a device of representation, but, more importantly, as a device of interpretation. On this view, the original position would not simply emerge from our considered judgments but would help us to formulate them. It would not only model "what we regard as fair conditions," but offer us an interpretation of what fair conditions can mean for us. Hence, it would not serve only in the way Rawls emphasizes "as a unifying idea by which our considered convictions at all levels of generality are brought to bear on one another so as to achieve greater mutual agreement and self-understanding."[15] It would serve also as an explicitly interpretive idea, as an idea through which we can emphasize some of our intuitions, relate them to one another in a particular way, and paint one picture of who we are. On this analysis, the original position would not simply articulate for us what the shared meanings are that are latent in our public political culture but would help to delineate a particular account of these meanings with the idea that this particular account could prove acceptable to us all.

This third interpretation of the point of the original position can be supported by the idea of an overlapping consensus. Although any conception of justice for a modern democratic society must be independent of all comprehensive moral, philosophical and religious doctrines, the hope is that "justice as fairness" can be supported "by a consensus including the opposing religious, philosophical and moral doctrines likely to thrive over generations in a society effectively regulated by that conception of justice."[16] For Rawls, the important claim here is that while his conception of justice rests exclusively on no comprehensive doctrine, those doctrines that can flourish in a democratic regime each possess internal grounds for accepting it. In other words, even though there may be differences in the internal grounds upon which each doctrine defends the conception of justice, each nonetheless can support it. As such the conception of justice is more than a *modus vivendi*. It neither reflects simply a compromise between comprehensive doctrines, nor is it justified in purely instrumental terms, as the conception that is necessary if individuals with different moral, religious and philosophical commitments are to live together. Rather, adherents of the different comprehensive doctrines that can thrive in a democratic regime are meant to be able to acknowledge the same conception of justice because it marks a point at which the different comprehensive doctrines can converge or intersect despite their differences in matters that do not involve the public political culture.

To be sure, the idea of an overlapping consensus remains somewhat confusing. Rawls's aim seemed to be to provide a conception of justice that could be justified independently of all comprehensive notions of the good and hence could also be neutral with regard to them. But, by a workable conception of justice, he now seems to mean one that allows for only some religious, philosophical and moral doctrines, even if these are the most likely to thrive "over generations in a society effectively regulated by that conception of justice." In what sense is the conception of justice independent of all comprehensive doctrines if we are to worry only about its acceptability with regard to certain *flourishing* comprehensive doctrines? Does this concern not violate the expanded principle of toleration with which Rawls begins his consideration of issues of justice? We do not, in fact, concede the "fact of pluralism." Instead, we provide a conception of justice that offers a limited pluralism in which some comprehensive doctrines and conceptions of the good are excluded.

Rawls does not deny this point. He admits that his political conception of justice for a democratic society might work against certain comprehensive doctrines; indeed, he admits that some of the comprehensive doctrines that might fail to thrive in a democratic society might include valuable conceptions of the good, which would then be lost to the society. Still he claims that, "No society can include within itself all forms of life." As he continues, "We may ... lament the limited space, as it were, of social worlds, and of ours in particular; and we may regret some of the inevitable effects of our culture and social structure ... But these social necessities are not to be mistaken for arbitrary bias or for injustice."[17] "Justice as fairness" is not meant to be all-inclusive; it is meant rather to give the society of which it is a part a stable point of convergence on matters of justice by presenting a reasonable interpretation of its political ideas and traditions.

To use Rawls's example, an overlapping consensus on "justice as fairness" might comprise three different doctrines. One is a religious view which accepts the conception of justice because its own ideas involve principles of toleration and hence support the liberties of a constitutional order. The second view is a comprehensive liberalism which supports the conception because it conforms to its own ideas of the person and of the value of human life. Finally, the third view affirms the conception of justice on strictly political grounds as that conception which is "sufficient to express political values that, under the reasonably favorable conditions that make a more or less just constitutional democracy possible, normally outweigh whatever other values may oppose them."[18] Although each of these views have different reasons for supporting the conception of justice, the crucial point for Rawls is that all can support it. It is not a conception to which the different positions merely accede or on which they compromise. Rather, by a conception of justice workable and practicable for us, Rawls means one that is acceptable because it can form part of whatever comprehensive doctrines and conceptions of the good democratic citizens can affirm. As Rawls writes, "Since we assume each citizen to affirm some such view or other, we hope to make it possible for all to accept the political conception as true, or as reasonable from the standpoint of their own comprehensive view, whatever it may be."[19] The groups who can support this conception will be able to do so for their own reasons in terms that preserve the distinctiveness and comprehensiveness of their general religious, philosophical or moral views. But this conception of justice will not include all possible conceptions of the good.

Model Conceptions

According to the account of Rawls's theory of justice as I have presented it thus far, the task of a conception of justice is to find a way of interpreting the strictly political meanings of the institutions, practices and traditions of a democratic society in a workable way so that conflicts over this meaning can be resolved; moreover, by a workable interpretation is meant one that is neutral with regard to the truth of any of the comprehensive doctrines that can flourish in a democratic society and that, therefore, can be supported by an overlapping consensus of them. The task of constructing such an interpretation requires developing certain model conceptions. In "Justice as Fairness: Political not Metaphysical," Rawls appeals to a more fundamental intuitive idea beneath the conflict between Lockean and Rousseauian interpretations of our tradition – namely, to the idea of "society as a system of fair social cooperation between free and equal persons." Similarly in "Kantian Constructivism in Moral Theory" he refers to the model conceptions of a well-ordered society and moral persons that are meant to picture the fundamental ideas, latent in our public political culture, of freedom and equality, social cooperation and moral personality. As our preceding discussion might suggest, these conceptions are not supposed to present the full extent or controversial aspects of these ideas; they are meant rather to define them in a way that all members of a democratic society can accept, whatever their idea of the good and whatever their differences over the full, extrapolitical meaning of the ideas at issue. As Rawls continues, "Whether the doctrine that eventually results fulfills its purpose is then decided by how it works out: once stated, it must articulate a suitable conception of ourselves and of our relation to society and connect this conception with workable first principles of justice, so that after due consideration, we can acknowledge the doctrine proposed."[20] It remains unclear whether Rawls's model conceptions do accomplish this task and, indeed, whether any model conceptions can. I shall look first at the idea of a well-ordered society.

The model conception of a well-ordered society is meant to highlight those features of social cooperation among free and equal persons that concern the role of justice in such cooperation. From this point of view, it is important, first, that the conception of justice is publicly known and generally acknowledged, that it effectively regulates the society and that the basic structure of the society complies with it. Second, it is important that social cooperation in a well-ordered society involves fair terms of cooperation. Those who cooperate with one another share common burdens and are to benefit in some appropriate way and, to this extent, fair terms of cooperation involve the idea of reciprocity and mutuality. Finally, the well-ordered society involves the idea of individual conceptions of the good whether these conceptions are the conceptions of single persons, groups, families or even nation-states. These ideas of the good or of "rational advantage" specify what each is trying to achieve through social cooperation. Rawls allows that there are other features of a well-ordered society. Nevertheless, these, he thinks, establish a fruitful model for reflecting on a political conception of justice for a democratic society and set up the goal for the choice of principles.

It is nonetheless striking that Rawls begins with the idea of social cooperation, for it is not clear that this idea exhausts all that politics or our political culture might mean for us. What, for instance, about the ideas of mutual deliberation and political participation? The idea of social cooperation, for Rawls, is not simply that of efficiently organized and coordinated social activity, nor is it restricted to the idea of providing rules as means to some overall end. Rather social cooperation centrally involves the idea of fair terms of cooperation and hence the ideas of reciprocity and mutuality in the sharing of burdens and benefits. We need not always cooperate only for mutual advantage; we can cooperate for altruistic reasons as well as for the good of the families, associations and communities to which we belong.

But the objection I am raising here is not that Rawls's conception of justice assumes the idea of a privatistic society or that social cooperation has a purely instrumental meaning.[21] Reciprocity and mutuality, however, also seem to have important, stronger senses than those involved in the sharing of burdens and benefits. They also seem to pertain to our idea of the possibility of free political self-definition. We cooperate for goals of our own or goals we hold in common. But politics also involves the setting of goals and the determination of both collective and individual aims and aspirations. Our social and political intercourse has a self-definitional function for us, as that arena in which we freely and deliberatively determine with one another who we are and what our rational advantage might be. Whatever the meaning of social cooperation does involve, it does not adequately represent this idea of politics as a domain of free and mutual self-definition.

Rawls would consider this idea to reflect an Aristotelian conception of politics and he would therefore preclude it as a basis for principles of justice in a pluralistic society because it forms part of a comprehensive moral doctrine. "Justice as fairness does not of course deny that some will find their most important good in political life and therefore that political life is central to their comprehensive good,"[22] but this attitude can have no part in a strictly political conception of justice for a democratic regime since not all democratic citizens need possess it. Still, against Rawls, one might argue that some version of an Aristotelian conception has come to form a dimension of our political traditions themselves and that it is therefore latent in our strictly political self-understandings. In other words, one might argue that if human beings cannot be considered essentially political animals for all moral and metaphysical purposes, nonetheless, part of the meaning of our democratic traditions is that the political domain itself involves a more robust and Aristotelian notion of politics than that modeled by the idea of social cooperation. Political society is at least also that domain in which we freely and equally deliberate with one another in determining what sort of people we are from a political point of view and what our political ideals and purposes ought to be. Hence, to define a well-ordered society from the outset in terms simply of cooperation is to make the conception of justice formulated to suit the society too one-sided from the start.

Again, a Rawlsian might reply that the conception is meant to be one-sided, that the idea of the model conception of a well-ordered society is not meant to represent all aspects of a democratic polity, but to represent those aspects on which we can achieve a workable agreement and that are important from the point of view of formulating a workable conception of justice for us. But this is precisely the goal that the model conception of a well-ordered society may not achieve. If we can insist on the importance to our conception of justice of the notions of free and equal deliberation and the free and equal political self-definition that is to issue from it, then it is at least not obvious that social cooperation is inclusive enough a category with which to begin. The same partiality seems to emerge from Rawls's idea of free and equal moral persons.

Rawls writes that a Kantian conception of justice asks "which traditionally recognized principles of freedom and equality, or which natural variations thereof, would free and equal moral persons themselves agree upon, if they were fairly represented solely as such persons and thought of themselves as citizens living a complete life in an on-going society?"[23] Naturally, this formulation of the question is circular if the problem with regard to ideas of freedom and equality is seen in deep hermeneutic terms, as a problem of what each means and hence what free and equal moral persons are. This is one of the instances in which Rawls writes as if the problem of pluralism were a problem simply of agreeing on principles and institutional arrangements to match our shared social meanings and in which he appears to overlook the question of how we ought to understand the meaning of freedom and equality or of free and equal moral persons themselves. Nonetheless this is presumably the question the model-conception of moral persons is meant to address.

Members of a well-ordered society are considered to be moral persons, Rawls claims, in that they possess two moral powers. They possess, first, a capacity for an effective sense of justice, by which Rawls means "the capacity to understand, to apply and to act from (and not merely in accordance with) principles of justice." Second, they possess a "capacity to form, to revise and rationally to pursue a conception of the good." In addition to these moral powers, moral persons are regarded as having two "highest-order" interests in developing and exercising these moral powers as well as one "higher-order" interest in "protecting and advancing" a particular conception of the good.[24] Behind the veil of ignorance, parties to the original position cannot know what their particular conception of the good is and are therefore motivated by a "thin theory of the good" or by a desire for primary goods. Nevertheless, the idea of moral persons as possessing the two highest-order desires together with a higher-order desire for some determinate good provides one of the poles around which a suitable conception of justice for a democratic society necessarily, according to Rawls, revolves.

It is worth emphasizing that this conception of moral persons is not itself supposed to constitute a full-fledged theory of the self. The characteristics of possessing a capacity for the two moral powers, a capacity for a determinate conception of the good, and an interest in primary goods are not meant to indicate what it means to be a person or what is essential to us as persons. Rather, they compose a description of moral personality that is restricted to the task of formulating principles of justice for a well-ordered society. Once we model essential characteristics of persons from the standpoint of justice and once we assume such persons are to choose principles of justice for a well-ordered society, we can use the idea of the original position as a bridge from one to the other. The structure of the original position models the equality of moral persons by requiring that the parties be situated symmetrically with respect to one another and hence that they choose principles of justice under identical conditions of ignorance. It models the freedom of moral persons by allowing these parties to choose under conditions of what Rawls calls rational autonomy. The parties are motivated in their choice of principles only by their highest- and higher-order desires to secure the conditions for realizing and exercising their moral powers and for pursuing their specific aims whatever they turn out to be. They are not motivated by any prior principles of justice or by anything other than their idea of rational advantage given the extensive "universalizing" limits on their knowledge.

Rawls distinguishes between this rational autonomy, which is an artificial characteristic of parties to the original position, inasmuch as they are conceived of as being motivated only by their rational desires, and the full autonomy of democratic citizens. Citizens express their full autonomy insofar as they not only act from the principles of justice but "understand these principles as issuing from a construction in which their conception of themselves as free and equal moral persons who are both reasonable and rational is adequately represented."[25] In other words, full autonomy means that democratic citizens can affirm the principles of justice because they can regard them as the results of a procedure that adequately mirrors the ideas of freedom and equality that are embedded in their public political culture.

But does this procedure adequately reflect these ideas? Even if we restrict ourselves to the point of view of justice, are the strictly political meanings freedom and equality have for us exhausted by the rational autonomy of moral persons, on the one hand, and by the "reasonable" constraints on the conditions for choice, on the other? Does our politically relevant conception of moral personality involve only the capacity for an effective sense of justice and the ability "to form, to revise and rationally to pursue a conception of the good?" My concern here is not Michael Sandel's worry that Rawls's conception of moral persons undermines a constitutive sense of the self by ignoring the substantive attachments and purposes people have which, for them, comprise their very identities.[26] Rawls does not deny that we can have aims, aspirations and loves without which we could not understand ourselves as we do understand ourselves, that we "would not, or could not, stand apart from."[27] The political restriction he places on the model conception of moral persons is meant to show that these attachments are simply not important from the point of view of formulating principles of justice.[28] In other words what matters from the point of view of justice is not our particular conceptions of the good or substantive attachments, but, instead, our ability to have conceptions of the good and to pursue and transform them. As Rawls writes,

> Citizens as free persons have the right to view their persons as independent and not identified with any particular system of ends. Given their moral power to form, to revise, and rationally to pursue a conception of the good, their public identity as a moral person and a self-originating source of claims is not affected by changes over time in their conceptions of the good...[29]

But if Sandel's concern is whether our substantive attachments of ideas of the good can be left out of the description of the choice of principles of justice, my concern is whether Rawls's political restriction is full enough, even if it is recognized as political restriction. Is the freedom and equality of moral persons that the original position models the only aspect of the meaning of freedom and equality that needs to be modeled?[30] Or is the importance of an idea of common deliberation again missing? Does the strictly political meaning of moral personhood not also involve a capacity for rational deliberation and self-definition? How is this capacity modeled in the idea of moral persons as characterized by their desires to develop and exercise highest- and higher order interests? How does such a capacity, if it is essential to a political idea of moral personhood enter into the idea of the original position? For Rawls, the situation of being constrained in one's choice of principles of justice by a veil of ignorance is a hypothetical situation that anyone can imaginatively enter into at any time. The virtue of the idea of such a veil is that whoever hypothetically situates himself or herself behind it and whenever he or she does so, the principles chosen remain the same. Hence, Rawls continues, the theory of justice can select one person at random to make the choice for everyone.

> We can, to make the circumstance more vivid, imagine that the parties are required to communicate with each other through a referee as intermediary and that he is to announce which alternatives have been suggested and the reasons offered in their support. He forbids the attempt to form coalitions, and he informs the parties when they have come to an understanding. But such a referee is actually superfluous, assuming that the deliberations of the parties must be similar.[31]

Just this notion of such isolated, rationally autonomous decisions seems to fail to model essential aspects of the idea of deliberation constitutive of the public traditions of a democratic society. For, if we are to justify norms and principles of justice to one another, these shared traditions would seem to include the idea of doing so in concert *with* one another. Of course Rawls allows for collective and informed deliberation at the stage of a constitutional convention which establishes the specific institutions of a democratic society. Of concern here, however, is the exclusion of such intersubjective deliberation at the initial stage of determining the principles of justice to be embodied in these institutions. As a device either of representation or interpretation, the original position is meant to model our deep political convictions and historical traditions. Instead, the original position instantiates only the perspective of Kant's categorical imperative according to which norms are justified according to what I can will for everyone as a universal law. It might be argued, however, that crucial to democratic justification is the idea that we all *together* will. In this regard, the starting point is not what I can accept under certain universalizing conditions as favorable to me from the perspective of my highest- and higher-order interests; it is rather or also what we can together accept through discussions oriented to understanding one another precisely in our different social and economic situations and with our different determinate conceptions of the good. If we want an adequate model of either moral personhood or the freedom and equality of moral persons, then, it is not clear that the idea of a fair but isolated choice is sufficient. Shared democratic understandings at least also seem to include notions of a free and equal communication with one another, communal processes of reflection and self-definition between free and equal citizens and common processes of deliberation over collective goals.

From this point of view, Rawls's remarks on the fair value of the political liberties are of some interest because they seem to indicate a more robust conception of the political meaning of free and equal moral persons than that pictured by the original position. The first principle of justice that Rawls thinks would be chosen in the original position now reads that "each person is to have an equal right to a fully adequate scheme of basic liberties which is compatible with a similar scheme of liberties for all." Hence citizens are to enjoy "freedom of thought and liberty of conscience; the political liberties and freedom of association as well as the freedoms specified by the liberty and integrity of the person and finally the rights and liberties covered by the rule of law."[32] Rawls distinguishes, in general, between the meaning of a liberty and its value or worth to individual citizens. While everyone has the same scheme of basic freedoms, the worth to each person of these freedoms can be affected by poverty, ignorance and a general lack of material means. Hence, while all citizens enjoy religious freedom, for example, the value of this freedom may be greater for those who also have the means to realize all tenets of their faith including, if necessary, regular religious pilgrimages to distant countries. The lesser worth of these basic liberties for others is meant to be compensated for by the second principle of justice, namely: first, that social and economic inequalities are to be attached to offices and positions open to all under conditions of fair equality of opportunity, and second, that they must be to the greatest benefit of the least advantaged members of society.[33] Hence, if some members of a religious faith are able more easily to satisfy its requirements or recommendations, the lesser ability of others of the same faith is justified on the grounds that were social and economic inequalities arranged differently, they would be even less able to satisfy the requirements of their faith.

Within this scheme, however, the equal political liberties have a special status. The unequal worth of political liberties cannot be sufficiently compensated for by the notion that if some citizens did not have a greater means for influencing the political process than others, these others would have even less means. The political process determines the laws and policies that regulate the basic structure of the society itself; to be fair it must be accessible to everyone affected by its decisions. Hence, the first principle of justice must guarantee not simply the formal freedoms of political choice and association; it must include their fair-value or equal worth as well. All must have a fair opportunity to hold public office and to influence the outcome of political decisions. The specific arrangements necessary to effect this guarantee, Rawls thinks, are beyond the scope of a conception of justice; nonetheless, he does claim that one guideline would seem to be "to keep political parties independent of large concentrations of private economic and social power in a private-property democracy, and of governmental control and bureaucratic power in a liberal socialist regime."[34]

If one neglects Rawls's focus here on political parties, his conception of guaranteeing the fair-value of the political liberties seems to be a step in the direction of recognizing the value of collective self-definition and political participation. The original position assures that the parties to it are free to make *individual* choices in their own rational interest, with regard to their own moral powers. But it does not itself seem to model the idea of *collective* choice through free and equal debate and argumentation or, in other words, the idea that in a democracy citizens come to a fully informed and rational agreement over principles of justice on the basis of a mutual and reciprocal understanding of one another's positions. In guaranteeing the fair-value of the political liberties, however, Rawls claims that "society must bear at least a large part of the cost of organizing and carrying out the political process and must regulate the conduct of elections." If elements of the political process include not simply the election of candidates from the major parties, but grass-roots organizing, voluntary associations, newspapers of all political perspectives, equal access of all groups to the media and so on, and if society must bear a large part of the cost of supporting these elements of the political process, then we seem to have precisely the more robust picture of politics that is missing from the idea of the original position itself.

Of course, Rawls emphasizes that the special status he accords to the political liberties is not to be justified on Aristotelian grounds. The fair-value of these liberties has to be guaranteed not because of the importance of politics in people's lives; on the contrary, he asserts, "Given the size of the modern state, the exercise of the political liberties is bound to have a lesser place in the conception of the good of most citizens than the exercise of the other basic liberties." The special status of the political liberties is rather justified on the grounds that it incorporates "into the basic structure of society the fair representation of persons achieved by the original position."[35] But if we take more seriously Rawls's idea of supporting the organization and carrying out of the political process, then the Aristotelian conception of politics, if not the value of politics for individual members of a modern society, would seem to be closer to his conception than he admits. Moreover, it becomes unclear why this conception should be simply a consequence of isolated choice in the original position as opposed to an element that the original position itself is to model.

If we are really to guarantee the fair-value of the political liberties, in fact, it is not clear that we do not have to guarantee the fair-value of at least some of the civil liberties as well. Rawls claims that to guarantee the fair-value of all the basic liberties would be socially divisive. Those whose religious beliefs required that they engaged in regular pilgrimages would demand the means to do so and would thus make larger claims on the material means of the society than those whose religious beliefs required no such expenses. However, if the fair-value of the political liberties requires not just a formal freedom to engage in the full political process, but a sufficiently equal means as well, then the guarantee of the fair-value of some other freedoms may need to be guaranteed as well. If freedom of conscience does not require the right to public support for religious pilgrimages it might involve the right to an equal education, for instance, so that all citizens have not only access to the instruments of the wider political process but the skills necessary to use them as well. This right might include greater economic and social reforms than those indicated by the difference principle defined, in general, in terms of the idea that any social and economic inequalities are to be arranged so that they are to the advantage of the least advantaged. The notion of free and equal political participation and deliberation seems to be as much a part of our public political culture as that of self-interested choice, even if we grant the conditions Rawls imposes on such self-interested choice. But if this free and equal political participation and deliberation is to be made possible, then we need not just the public financing of elections, but also the full conditions for an open, active and revitalized public domain including an educated and informed public and a population not preoccupied with questions of material and economic survival.

Such questions about the selectivity of Rawls's model conceptions and even of his account of the fair-value of the political liberties reflect only one different perspective one might take on the meaning of our public political culture. From another, equally democratic, point of view, it might be argued that what is most significant about our shared political traditions are notions of minimal government, economic self-sufficiency and the equation of social rewards with the extent, quality and social usefulness of one's labor. According to this interpretation of the meaning of our political traditions, Rawls's model conceptions must be illegitimate because they issue in a completely unjustifiable second part of the second principle of justice: namely, that social and economic inequalities must be arranged to advantage the least advantaged. Parties to the original position behind a veil of ignorance would choose the difference principle, Rawls claims, because it maximizes their chances of being satisfied with the principles of justice whatever their social and economic, status and conception of the good may turn out to be. But a libertarian might argue that if parties to the original position would choose such a principle, there must be something wrong with the conception of the original position. The shared understandings of a democratic political culture centrally involve the idea that government is an instrument for assisting the individual in his or her pursuits; it is not an instrument for taxing individuals out of the just rewards for their labor or a means of redistributing the wealth of the society. It is rather meant to be as non-existent and unobtrusive as possible, a last resort for self-sufficient individuals when their claims conflict with those of others. Any "modeling" of the meanings embedded in our political culture that fails to emphasize this kind of stalwart individualism can neither claim to have adequately represented those meanings or hope for the approval of an overlapping consensus.

Even if we recognize these alternative interpretations of the meaning of our public political culture, it might seem that both Aristotelian and libertarian objections pertain to the details of Rawls model conceptions rather than to the idea of model conceptions in general or to the notion of a pragmatic, political hermeneutics. One might argue that although Rawls may have failed in his attempt to articulate the political conception of justice that is most reasonable for us, his pragmatically hermeneutic tactics are none-theless the correct tactics for an approach to issues of justice. More-over, one might argue that our task is simply to formulate a more adequate model of our political traditions, one which can be sup-ported by an overlapping consensus, if Rawls's own cannot. But if this more adequate model must be fashioned out of the three dis-parate perspectives on liberal democratic traditions that we have considered — those of Rawlsian liberalism, Aristotelian politics and Nozickean libertarianism — it is not clear how. The interpretations do not differ over conceptions of the good nor do they involve dif-ferent comprehensive moral doctrines; they differ precisely over the best way to understand what the meaning is that is latent in our public political culture. Rather than giving us a picture of that cul-ture that we can all accept, each gives us a picture that excludes the others and by so doing threatens its own acceptance by an overlapping consensus.

Here the problem we raised in the last chapter with regard to dif-fering interpretations of our medical care practices arises with regard to our political traditions as a whole. Even if we take a prag-matic approach and try to find a conception of justice that is simply workable for us given our political traditions, we can have different notions of what those political traditions most pragmatically might mean and hence, just what conception will be workable or most reasonable for us. Indeed, the question arises as to whether a prag-matically adequate picture of our political traditions would not have to contain all the differences in the interpretation of those traditions that the idea of model conceptions was designed to re-solve. If we understand our political traditions differently, then we might understand the point of viable intersection for an overlap-ping consensus differently as well and any attempt to establish principles of justice based on just one of these intersections will violate other possible, strictly political interpretations.

This objection to Rawls's conception of justice, then, is not simply that it is one-sided, that it depicts only one aspect of our shared political traditions. Rawls's interpretive starting point is that any attempt to model our political traditions will necessarily be one-sided; it will not present a full picture of our democratic tradi-tions but will rather offer an appropriate picture of them from the standpoint of achieving an overlapping consensus. Yet, Rawls's model conceptions may just be too one-sided to accomplish the pragmatic task he sets for them. They appear not simply to leave out certain aspects of our traditions or to regard these aspects as secondary; rather, they seem to leave out and regard as secondary precisely those aspects of our traditions that different model conceptions would regard as primary. Nor is it obvious that any model conception other than those Rawls articulates would be able to gain the support of an overlapping consensus. Rather, it is arguable that any hermeneutic picture of a shared political culture will have simply to enter into a series of interpretive debates in which citizens themselves discuss the meaning of their history and traditions. Such hermeneutic pictures will simply offer partisan views as, in the end, Walzer does and they will have to defend these views on some basis other than that they supply the basis of an overlapping consensus.

If we give up on the attempt to forge such a consensus, however, the question I raised at the end of the last chapter arises again somewhat more forcefully. If we abandon the attempt to forge even an overlapping consensus directed only at a pragmatic convergence of our strictly political views, what can a hermeneutic approach to issues of justice hope to accomplish? In his discussion of public reason, Rawls briefly hints at a kind of answer we might give.

The Idea of Public Reason

Rawls claims that the notion of free public reason is an "essential companion" to a political conception of justice. Public reason involves both common conceptions of the good of moral persons (leading to Rawls's idea of primary goods) and the idea of publicity, the idea that knowledge of the principles of justice and their justification must be available to all citizens. But it also involves the application of principles of justice. While the political conception of justice specifies what these principles are, we also need "certain guidelines of inquiry and publicly recognized rules of assessment" to determine how to apply them. According to Rawls, "Agreement on a conception of justice is worthless — not an effective agreement at all — without agreement on these further matters." Moreover, "given the fact of pluralism there is ... no better practicable alternative than to limit ourselves to the shared methods of, and the public knowledge available to, common sense, and the procedures and conclusions of science when these are not controversial. It is these shared methods and this common knowledge that allows us to speak of public reason."[36]

The appeal here to common sense and the non-controversial conclusions of science is meant to accomplish for the question of applying the conception of justice what the appeal to our public political culture was meant to accomplish for formulating the conception: namely, recourse to a nexus of shared understandings that neutralizes the effects of substantive differences over moral, religious and philosophical doctrine and conceptions of the good. But the same problem we have been considering with regard to formulating a conception of justice arises also with regard to applying it. If citizens can differ in their understandings of the meaning of their political traditions and culture – if, indeed, they can differ on what they take to be an acceptable picture of their political traditions and culture – they can also differ on their understanding of both what common sense requires and what conclusions of science are non-controversial. Indeed, it would seem that some of our fiercest political debates develop in this area: debates over the effects of global warming or whether it occurs at all, and hence what a society's obligations to a world population are, or debates over when life begins or over the secondary effects of smoking or debates over what constitutes *per se* negligence or race or sex discrimination. If citizens cannot simply rely on the meanings embedded in their public political culture to resolve conflicts over appropriate political principles and arrangements because these meanings can be differently interpreted, it also seems evident that they cannot simply appeal to common sense or to a public reason because they can differ here as well.

In fact, however, just this possibility of differing seems to be at least one of Rawls's reasons for looking to public reason. Public reason contrasts with the forms of reasoning that belong to comprehensive moral, religious and philosophical doctrines and because it contrasts with these forms of reasoning it allows for change and development in a way that they do not. Rawls compares the rationale behind the limitations Rousseau and Locke place on the liberty of conscience to the rationale for the same limitations imposed by Aquinas and the Protestant reformers. For Aquinas, different religions are matters of heresy and cannot be tolerated because they endanger the life of the soul. Indeed, Aquinas supported the death penalty for heretics on the grounds that a corruption of faith was a much more serious matter than other crimes for which the death penalty was already imposed. In contrast, Rousseau and Locke thought religious freedom had to be limited simply because of the threats it seemed to pose to the public order. "If Catholics and atheists were not to be tolerated it was because it seemed evident that such persons could not be relied upon to observe the bonds of civil society."[37]

For Rawls, the form of this limitation is important because it allows for alteration through a "greater historical experience and a knowledge of the wider possibilities of political life." Aquinas's judgment is based not on common expectations with regard to what Catholics and atheists can be expected to do but on faith and is therefore dogmatic. In contrast "[w]hen the denial of liberty is justified by an appeal to public order as evidenced by common sense, it is always possible to urge that the limits have been drawn incorrectly, that experience does not in fact justify the restriction."[38] In other words, because what counts as public reason has an interpretive dimension the appeal to it allows for change and even development where a reliance on comprehensive doctrines does not.

The same line of reasoning, it seems to me, might be applied not simply to the application of principles of justice but to the model conceptions of a well-ordered society, the original position and moral persons in terms of which these principles are formulated. In other words, it might be argued that while we might draw different and contending model conceptions from our public political culture, it is important that these are rival pictures of what our traditions mean and not rival philosophical, moral or religious doctrines. If I know my conception of justice to be based on comprehensive moral truth, then I can reject the possible validity of any other conception of justice and can refuse to reconsider my own. When, however, I understand my conception as simply an interpretation of the meanings embedded in my political and historical traditions, then I must allow both for the possibility of other interpretations and for the possibility that my own might be enriched by the insights of others into dimensions of meaning I may not have stressed. In "The Idea of an Overlapping Consensus" Rawls himself writes that "more than one political conception may be worked up from the fund of shared political ideas." Moreover, he claims that "this is desirable, as these rival conceptions will then compete for citizens' allegiance and be gradually modified and deepened by the contest between them."[39] But the same might be said not simply for the political conceptions worked up from the fund of shared political ideas, but for our ideas of the meaning of the fund of shared political ideas itself. If these compete for citizens' allegiance then they too can be "modified and deepened by the contest between them." In a later chapter I shall be calling this notion that of a hermeneutic conversation. First, however, I want to look at Ronald Dworkin's account of legal interpretation as a means of achieving greater clarity on what a hermeneutic approach to questions of justice might involve.

4

LEGAL INTERPRETATION AND
CONSTRAINT

The question we have been considering concerns the question of subjectivism or the question, as we can now understand it, of the possibility of achieving an interpretive consensus on either our shared social meanings or a pragmatically appropriate understanding of them. If our principles of justice are to rest on what might be called holistic understandings of our important political traditions and social convictions, can we agree on what the proper or even workable holistic understandings are? We have considered plausible interpretations of our medical care practices that differ from the one Walzer offers. Moreover, we have seen that even if a hermeneutic understanding of a political culture is given an explicitly pragmatic dimension, we can differ in our ideas of the elements that a suitable, pragmatic understanding must include. We can understand our political culture at least in the very different terms of Rawlsian liberalism, a more robust and participatory concept of the meaning of democratic politics or a Nozickean libertarianism. One problem with a hermeneutic political theory thus seems to be that it must encounter the same diversity of interpretations that occurs in the humanities. But while diversity in the humanities may be admissible and even productive, it is not clear how it can be either with regard to political theory. Rather, it might seem that, here, we must be able to agree on shared social meanings so that we can agree on the principles, actions and practices that are appropriate to them.

One way to pursue this issue is to examine the structure of legal interpretation in a democratic society since, in adjudicating particular cases, the legal system seems to provide for just the kind of interpretive decisiveness we need to determine suitable principles, practices and actions for us. The courts decide cases, and in so doing they not only resolve conflicts and disagreements over individual actions and practices; they also decide the interpretive questions of which law is relevant to a particular case, how that law is relevant and how the evidence, precedents and law are themselves to be understood. Of course, according to some "legal realist" accounts of the law, this interpretive decisiveness is itself arbitrary; judges interpret the meaning of laws, precedents and the text of the Constitution in line with their personal political prejudices or even in line with temporary whims and feelings.[1] The legal theorists that are interesting from the point of view of developing a hermeneutic approach to issues of justice, however, are those who try to discover within the process of legal interpretation a set of constraints that can lift a judge's understanding of the law above the simply personal and subjective.

These theorists do not claim that such constraints can eliminate all differences in the way different judges may decide cases. They argue, instead, that there are standards for the validity of legal interpretations — procedures and a hierarchy of authority for resolving disputes in the law — that render such differences manageable. Hence, as Owen Fiss explains, although there may be many different schools of literary interpretation, "in legal interpretation there is only one school and attendance is mandatory."[2] I shall look first at Ronald Dworkin's analysis of the kind of constraint that he thinks is promoted by this one school. Much of what he says helps confirm and develop the hermeneutic account we have examined thus far with regard to criteria for interpretive adequacy, the role of an understanding of intentions and the tasks of the interpreter. At the same time, Dworkin's interpretations of particular cases betray certain reservations about a full-scale hermeneutic approach to the law. Although these reservations remain largely unacknowledged in his own work, it will be useful to explore them as a means of illuminating both the merits and the dangers of a hermeneutic approach not just to the law but to issues of justice in general. I shall begin by examining the analogy Dworkin establishes between literary and legal interpretation in the idea of writing a chain novel.

Law as Integrity

A chain novel is a novel written by a group of people rather than a single author in which each writer in the group is responsible for one chapter of the book. One person writes a first chapter and sends it to the person who is to write the second chapter. This second writer reads the first chapter, continues on its plot and themes in a new chapter and sends both chapters to a third person who reads them and writes a third chapter, that further develops the story. The writing goes on in this way until the entire group has written a chapter and the novel is completed. For Dworkin, the important similarity between this exercise and the law is that each author after the first has the same two responsibilities as does the judge. Each author must both create a piece of work and develop or continue on the work of others just as each judge must both offer an opinion on a new case and adhere to the pre-existing meaning of the relevant law. Each new chapter, then, must be both a new creation and a further chapter in a single book and this means that each author must understand the meaning of the parts of the book that have already been written so that the new parts he or she writes will serve to continue the same book that the first novelist began. Similarly, each judge must both decide a new case and decide it in a way consistent with the meaning the law already has. How does either judge or author accomplish this task?

From the Hirschean perspective we noted in chapter 2, it might seem obvious that a second writer in a line of the chain novelists must look for the intention the first writer had in writing the beginning parts of the book. The second writer would then be able to carry out the same intention and the third writer could then discern the single intention of the first two authors and further carry out that single intention in his or her chapter of the book. This process of discerning and carrying out the original intention would continue until the book was finished and the book would thus be unified as a completed representation of a single literary intention. The implications of this account of the interpretive task for the law are clear. On this view, a judge can claim to be advancing the rule of a specific law only if he holds to the original intention of the legislators in passing it. Judges deciding the cases falling under the law could be said to be furthering the law and carrying it out only if they reiterated in their decisions the single intention at the law's origin.

Dworkin dismisses this account of the chain novelist's and judge's interpretive task for much the same reason we rejected Hirsch's argument for deferring to an author's intentions in chapter 2. Dworkin does not deny that one might conceive of the task of interpretation as that of ascertaining an author's or legislator's intentions, that if one were the second in a line of chain novelists one might want to know what the first author had intended to create or that a judge might be interested in a legislator's wishes with regard to a law. But, the attempt to understand intentions does not guarantee objectivity in interpretation because intentions, as Dworkin puts this point, are complex. They must always be described and they can be conceivably described in different ways. If we argue, for example, that any adequate interpretation of a particular poem by Wordsworth must consider his intentions in writing it, we still have to understand and describe those intentions. We have to determine which of Wordsworth's myriad intentions or which aspect of which intentions at the time he wrote the poem might have been relevant to his work; we have to decide how the intentions or aspects of intentions we select are relevant to the written text and we have to read the meaning of the written text itself in a certain way so that we can show how the intentions we have settled on are reflected in it. Different interpreters can resolve these interpretive decisions and determinations in different ways. They can take different events and experiences in Wordsworth's life to be significant, refer to different pieces of textual and extratextual evidence and integrate all the different pieces of evidence they take to be relevant in different ways. Dworkin cites the problem of the intentions of the framers of the Fourteenth Amendment with regard to the question of the constitutionality of the racial segregation of schoolchildren in the United States:

> Suppose a delegate to a constitutional convention votes for a clause guaranteeing equality of treatment, without regard to race, in matters touching people's fundamental interests; but he thinks that education is not a matter of fundamental interest and so does not believe that the clause makes racially segregated schools unconstitutional ... the delegate intends to prohibit discrimination in whatever in fact is of fundamental interest and also intends not to prohibit segregated schools.[3]

As Dworkin suggests, which intention we take as fundamental in this case will be decisive for our judgment of the legality of segregated education. If we take as primary the first half of the intention, namely that of guaranteeing equality of treatment in matters of fundamental importance, then we can outlaw segregated schools and still claim to be carrying out the delegate's intention under circumstances in which we recognize education to be of fundamental importance. If we take the second half of the intention to be primary, namely that of intending not to prohibit segregated schools, and if we still claim to be following the delegate's intention, then we cannot view such schools as constitutionally prohibited even if they preclude an equal treatment of blacks and whites. In either case we are engaged in a hermeneutic enterprise. We have to interpret the delegate's thoughts and motives, decide which elements within them are most important and order them in a meaningful way. We also have to determine which thoughts and motives made their way into the amendment as written and which evidence for this determination is relevant. The appeal to intentions thus does not provide us with a standard for the objectivity of interpretation. It rather simply offers us another text to be understood, a text that, because of our interpretive decisions, we may legitimately understand differently from others.

One might object here that intentions are actually not always complex. Dworkin does not consider such a case, but suppose the delegate to the constitutional convention intended simply to guarantee equal treatment in matters of fundamental importance and had no thoughts – hence, no intentions – at all with regard to the status of education as a matter of fundamental importance. The problem for the court would remain the same. Its task remains that of applying the law to the case of segregated education and, even if it conceived of this task as involving some understanding of the intentions of the framers of the Fourteenth Amendment, it would still have to interpret the meaning of those intentions for this case. In other words, it would have to reconstruct from its understanding of the intentions the delegate did have what his or her intentions with regard to the issue of segregated education would have been. Perhaps in 1868 education was not a matter of fundamental interest. Nevertheless, even if the court were to take an understanding of intentions as its primary interpretive focus, the question it has to decide is what the intention to guarantee equal treatment in matters of fundamental interest implies for the circumstances in which education is of fundamental interest because it helps determine life prospects and social circumstances.

The task of applying what we interpret as the delegates' intentions to these circumstances will be a complex one and will involve deciding how to understand the complex meaning of an intention to promote equal treatment under different circumstances and in different domains of life, the importance and role of which can change under different historical circumstances. Hence, even if we take a single aspect of an author's, legislator's or delegate's intention as the basis of our legal decisions, we cannot avoid the necessity of making interpretive decisions. In the case of writing a chain novel, if we focus on the original author's intentions we must decide how to advance what we take to be these intentions through further plot and character developments; in the case of law, we must determine what an author's or agent's original intentions might mean for the issues with which we must contend.[4] Just as the chain novelist must continue a text already begun, the judge must continue the enterprise of the law, carrying out its meaning but applying the law to new circumstances. It may be that the judge cannot simply create new law; neither can he or she'avoid interpretive decisions by appealing to a set of original intentions that are supposed not themselves to raise issues of interpretation.

If the appeal to an original intention cannot itself provide for the validity of an interpretation, what are the standards by which we can judge its validity? In discussing the validity of textual understanding, Dworkin points to the standard of "fit." The chain novelist must find an interpretation of the meaning of the text that can cover all or most of the elements of the text under study and show how they work together to compose a unified whole. Dworkin's idea here seems to be close to the ideas of internal coherence and consistency that the hermeneutic tradition has emphasized. That is, one must try to find an interpretation of textual meaning that can unify all the various parts of the text, an interpretation that can show, for instance, how the various traits of a character work to further the themes of the text or how a subplot fits in with the main plot. An interpretation need not encompass every aspect of a text. From the vantage point it offers, it may be necessary to see certain arguments, tropes and images as either irrelevant or, indeed, mistakes. Nonetheless, such a determination depends upon a general interpretation that can attribute some overall meaning to the text and can thereby offer a perspective from which inconsistent themes and arguments can be understood as inconsistent. If, however, the interpretation one favors requires that large sections of the text be understood as deviations from its overall point, then for Dworkin, as for the hermeneutic tradition in general, this interpretation is necessarily suspect. The interpretation must cover or fit a significant enough extent of the text that the text as written does not become one large irrelevance to a smaller theme.

How do we determine when an apparently irrelevant section is too large? The problem Dworkin raises at this point in his argument is the one we have been considering as to whether it is not possible to understand the coherence of a text or such text analogues as social meanings in different ways. Suppose a chain novelist can arrive at two different interpretations of the previous chapters of the novel, both of which "fit" to the same degree. Suppose, as Dworkin imagines, the chain novel at issue is the first part of Dickens's *A Christmas Carol*, now conceived of as having been written by a series of different authors. And suppose, as thus far written, two interpretations of the Scrooge character "fit" the text equally well, one interpretation according to which he is innately evil and one according to which he is socially corrupted by false, capitalistic values. As the standard for adjudicating between these two equally well-fitting interpretations, Dworkin introduces the idea of the "aesthetic hypothesis" or, in general, the standard of "best light." In trying to decide between two possible interpretations of the meaning of a work of art or of a social practice such as the law, the interpreter must decide which reveals the work or practice to be the best instance it can be of the "form or genre to which it is taken to belong."[5] In the case of interpreting the character of Scrooge, then, the chain novelist decides "which way of reading (or speaking or direction or acting) the text reveals it as the best work of art."[6] Or, in other words, which of the two interpretations in question will result in a better novel. He or she then continues the novel in such a way that this meaning is developed.

It is important to Dworkin's conception that the interpretation in terms of the standard of "best light" is a complicated one. In the case of *A Christmas Carol*, it may depend, in the first instance, upon substantive beliefs the chain novelist has about whether evil is innate or socially conditioned. But it also depends upon a series of formal convictions about how plots are best integrated with imagery, language and setting and which of these and other features of a book are more crucial to its being a good book. As Dworkin points out, one might conclude that "the original sin reading is much the more accurate depiction of human nature" but that the sociorealist reading provides *A Christmas Carol* with a deeper story as well as a more interesting formal structure as a whole.[7] In this case, one has to ask which reading makes the book better as a whole and, indeed, what ought to have priority in literature in general: formal structure or faithfulness to human nature. We can differ in our conclusions on both these issues and Dworkin insists that that these differences will be connected to our differing aesthetic theories and values. Indeed, we can differ in our views of both how a particular novel is to be understood as the best that it can be and "how good that is."[8] Nonetheless, our differing interpretations will all be "constrained," according to Dworkin, to the extent that they comply, first, with the standard of "fit" and, second, with that of "best light" as we understand it according to our aesthetic values.

The standards of fit and best light offer an additional constraint insofar as Dworkin means them to play off one another. His model here is contemporary accounts of the relation of theory and observation in science. The objectivity of natural science is no longer thought to consist in a simple correspondence between beliefs we have about the world and a theory-independent reality. Rather, the reality about which we have beliefs is already an interpreted reality, a reality that is already dependent upon a particular theoretical structure. The Quinian notion of a web of belief is thus the idea that this theoretical structure, "the entire body of our convictions about logic, mathematics, physics, and the rest," relates to our experience as an interdependent system and that we can revise any part of the web as long as we are willing to revise the other aspects of the web it would affect. As Dworkin continues, "If we held very different beliefs about the theoretical parts of physics and the other sciences we would, in consequence, divide the world into very different entities and the facts we 'encountered' about these different entities would be very different from the facts we now take to be unassailable." Yet this Quinian analysis does not mean that we can no longer test our hypotheses about the world at all. Instead, the point of Quine's conception, for Dworkin, is that we test these hypotheses in a complicated way, by checking and balancing different theoretical commitments and observations at varying levels of generality in an effort to discover the explanation of a phenomenon that is adequate to our experience as we come to conceive of it as a whole.[9]

Dworkin contends that the constraints on textual interpretation operate in a similar way. The various formal and substantive ideas involved in textual interpretation form a differentiated web of belief. Our beliefs about how the various contents of a text best cohere with one another to form a unified meaning can thus serve as a check on what formal structure, ideas of plot, imagery, unity and the like we can attribute to the text and, similarly, our aesthetic ideas set constraints on the ideas we can sanction of the text's substantive content. For example, it may not be open to us to understand an Agatha Christie novel as a philosophical disquisition on death even if, according to our aesthetic ideas, philosophical disquisitions on death are more valuable as pieces of literature than are mystery novels. If one tries to impose one's formal ideas of value on content in this way that content becomes a "shambles," Dworkin writes. "All but one or two of the sentences would be irrelevant to the supposed theme."[10]

In this sense, the criterion of fit, the idea that any adequate interpretation must be able to cover the greater part of the text, provides a check on the criteria of value or best light in terms of which we can understand it. Conversely, there are certain substantive meanings we might attribute to the text according to which its organization, style and structure would lose their aesthetic value. Both the content and the form of an Agatha Christie novel are the best they can be when they are understood in terms of the genre of a mystery novel and we come to this conclusion not only by applying the standards of fit and best light but by testing them against one another and achieving a kind of reflective equilibrium between them. Our substantive interpretation of content provides a check, in this case, on the formal aesthetic values we can impose on the text and the idea of what genre places the text in its best light constrains the meaning we can attribute to imagery, character development and plot. To the extent that our interpretation of the text complies with these requirements then, for Dworkin, it is constrained and valid, even if it cannot be considered uniquely correct.

In moving to the case of legal interpretation, Dworkin argues that the standards of fit and best light have obvious application. The judge must first find an interpretation of a body of law that "fits" it in the sense that it shows how a particular set of legal decisions work together to provide for a consistent legal understanding and adjudication of cases. This consistency, however, is not a superficial one. The idea is not simply to repeat past decisions, so that, for example, in 1954 the Supreme Court would have to uphold the whole of the 1896 decision in *Plessy v. Ferguson* and maintain separate educational facilities for whites and blacks. For Dworkin, law is integrity and this means that the judge in searching for the continuity in a series of cases must consider not only the criterion of fit but the standard of best light as well. In the case of the law, this means that he or she must both look for the continuity of principle that underlies the different decisions and choose between different possible interpretive principles by finding that principle or set of principles that allows the legal practice to be the best it can be. Integrity, Dworkin suggests is a virtue for political institutions as a whole. It

> demands that the public standards of the community be both made and seen, so far as this is possible, to express a single coherent scheme of justice and fairness in the right relation. An institution that accepts that ideal will sometimes, for that reason, depart from a narrow line of past decisions in search of a fidelity to principles conceived as more fundamental to the scheme as a whole.[11]

Just as in the case of textual interpretation, we may differ in our views of what makes of the past decisions and precedents the most coherent and best law it can be. Here, these differences issue from the judge's moral and political intuitions as to how the decisions and precedents in question can be understood to represent the best possible unifying law and principle, given the material. Hence our political differences will enter into our legal judgments and these may therefore differ just as our aesthetic judgments may differ. Still, our legal interpretations will be as constrained and objective as they can be, according to Dworkin, insofar as they appeal to the standards of fit and best light and insofar as the different levels involved in the standards of fit and best light provide the same kind of check on one another that the varying levels of our interpretation provide in the case of our understanding of works of art.

This idea, which Dworkin calls that of law as integrity, seems close to the general approach both Walzer and Rawls take towards issues of justice. The idea is to construct a general picture of the legal norms and fundamental legal convictions of a particular democratic society, to uncover the basic logic of a particular legal system and to use this logic as a normative framework that can serve as a guide for assessing and providing legal decisions. Indeed, for Dworkin this idea of integrity, of a non-superficial, principled coherence, issues itself from an interpretation of democratic practice as a third virtue in addition to those of justice and equality. Democracies do not accept what he calls "checkerboard" solutions to disputes over issues of justice or morality. They do not and could not accept as a viable compromise on the issue of abortion, for example, a solution that makes abortion illegal for pregnant women who are born in even years and legal for pregnant women born in odd ones.[12] Such a solution might seem fair to the different intuitions of pro-choice and pro-life advocates insofar as it takes each seriously and tries to accommodate both. It also seems just from each perspective at least in comparison to the worst-case scenario for each group. Pro-choice advocates could know that at least some women were allowed the choice they thought just and pro-life advocates could similarly know that at least half the cases of injustice against fetuses had been stopped.

Since we therefore cannot rule out checkerboard solutions on grounds of either fairness or justice, Dworkin contends that we do so on the basis of a third political virtue, namely integrity or the idea that we cannot treat people differently "where no principle can justify the distinction." In devising checkerboard solutions, he continues, "the state lacks integrity because it must endorse principles to justify part of what it has done that it must reject to justify the rest."[13] The United States has often done precisely this: it tried to find a compromise on the issue of slavery by counting a slave as three-fifths of a person, for example, and, along with other democracies, it has always enacted and enforced laws that are coherent in themselves but cannot constitute together a coherent set of principles. Nonetheless, integrity remains an ideal rooted in the political morality of societies governed by law. It is part of that morality that "the community as a whole and not just individual officials one by one must act in a principled way"[14] and, to this extent, the hermeneutic precepts of fit, internal coherence and best light are part of our conception of the kind of principled community we seek to be.

Dworkin himself does not appear to be completely content with such a staunchly hermeneutic vision. Rather, in his interpretations of specific cases in British and American law, he applies his hermeneutic theory rather differently than his accounts of both literary interpretation and law as integrity would lead one to expect. I shall consider two of these interpretations; first, his account of the personal injury case of *McLoughlin v. O'Brian* and, second, his analysis of *Brown v. Board of Education.*

McLoughlin and Brown

In the case, *McLoughlin v. O'Brian*, Mrs McLoughlin sued Mr O'Brian for emotional injuries she suffered as a consequence of learning that Mr. O'Brian's car had hit Mr McLoughlin's car, killing one of his children and injuring both Mr McLoughlin and the other three children. Mrs McLoughlin heard about the accident two hours after it happened and, upon arriving at the hospital and seeing the condition of her family, went into nervous shock. The precedents discussed at the trial all involved cases in which plaintiffs recovered for emotional injuries that they had suffered at the scene of the accident. The question for the judge in *McLoughlin v. O'Brian* was whether Mrs McLoughlin could recover given that the injury did not occur at either the scene or the time of the accident. Dworkin's question is how an ideal judge, whom he names Hercules, with ample intelligence and no time limitations would decide the case.

Hercules, Dworkin claims, "must find, if he can, some coherent theory about legal rights to compensation for emotional injury such that a single political official with that theory could have reached most of the results the precedents report."[15] He considers six such theories:

> (1) No one has a moral right to compensation except for physical injury. (2) People have a moral right to compensation for emotional injury suffered at the scene of an accident against anyone whose carelessness caused the accident but have no right to compensation for

emotional injury suffered later. (3) People should recover compensation for emotional injury when a practice of requiring compensation in their circumstances would diminish the overall costs of accidents or otherwise make the community richer in the long run. (4) People have a moral right to compensation for any injury, emotional or physical, that is the direct consequence of careless conduct, no matter how unlikely or unforeseeable it is that that conduct would result in that injury. (5) People have a moral right to compensation for emotional or physical injury that is the consequence of careless conduct, but only if that injury was reasonably foreseeable by the person who acted carelessly. (6) People have a moral right to compensation for reasonably foreseeable injury but not in circumstances when recognizing such a right would impose massive and destructive financial burdens on people who have been careless out of proportion to their moral fault.[16]

These statements contradict one another, according to Dworkin. If Hercules decides on either (1) or (2) he must settle the case in favor of Mr O'Brian; if he decides on (4) he must find for Mrs McLoughlin. (3) requires an economic calculation, (5) a judgment about foreseeability and (6) a judgment both about foreseeability and financial burdens.

Dworkin argues that statement (1) can be dismissed immediately because it cannot cover the relevant past decisions. Hercules also dismisses statement (2) immediately on the grounds that it fails to state a principle of justice at all. As Dworkin continues, "It draws a line that it leaves arbitrary and unconnected to any more general moral or political consideration"[17] and he suggests that the same may be true of statement (3). Principles (4),(5) and (6) require more thought. Dworkin proposes as a hypothetical that the history of cases does not support or "fit" (4) and that this history "fits" (5) and (6) equally well. In order to decide between (5) and (6), then, Hercules must look to the standard of best light and the issue here, according to Dworkin, is "which interpretation shows the legal record to be the best it can be from the standpoint of substantive political morality." Is this record seen in a better light if it is seen as by and large "enforcing the principle of forseeability as its test for moral responsibility for damage caused by negligence" or if it is seen as by and large "enforcing the principle of forseeability limited by some overall ceiling on liability."[18] Hercules's answer will depend upon his own moral and political convictions, Dworkin claims, and, in particular, it will depend on how he relates the virtues of justice and fairness to one another as part of law as integrity. For instance, he may himself believe that the second test is more just but think that the first conforms better to the public view and hence that, given the circumstances, a decision in line with this test is fairer. He may also think that the first is better in this case because of its conformity with public values but that in other cases, such as *Brown v. Board of Education*, more important matters are at stake, matters that therefore cannot be left to popular morality.

At first glance, it may not be clear why the option of deferring to popular morality is open to Hercules at all. If his consideration of the legal record in terms of its internal coherence and as the best it can be indicates to him that a principle such as (6) serves as its unifying principle, then it would seem, from an interpretive point of view, that he ought to settle the case in this way. Trying, instead, to align the immanent meaning of the legal history with popular opinion seems to be analogous to the circumstance in which a literary critic might try to claim, on the one hand, that in his view *A Christmas Carol* is sentimental tripe about a foolish old man but, on the other, that since popular opinion considers it a classical critique of capitalistic values he intends to understand it in this way as well. If law is interpretive, as Dworkin claims, then the task of the judge would appear to be that of interpreting the legal record, just as the literary critic's task is that of interpreting the literary text. Neither task would seem to involve either surveying and interpreting public opinion or conforming one's understanding of meaning to it.

Dworkin might reply to this objection that the idea of fairness is itself part of law as integrity. In looking to the values of the community, the judge is not simply succumbing to political pressures but interpreting the law in terms of an inclusive idea of the principles and values of the society. As Dworkin explains, an inclusive integrity means that the judge "constructs his overall theory of present law so that it reflects, so far as possible, coherent principles of fairness, substantive justice, and procedural due process and reflects these combined in the right relation."[19] Principles of fairness involve the political procedures that distribute political power in the right way; the question of substantive justice is a question of the decisions that a political system ought to make about distributing goods and resources and the question of due process is a question of the right procedures for determining whether a citizen has violated the law. In looking for an inclusive integrity then, Hercules might opt for interpretation (5) because it supplies an interpretation more in line with the integrity of the community as a whole than that supplied by (6). Its articulation of the role of the judiciary and, hence, the relation of substantive justice and fairness is more consistent with all the other considerations the society must bring into its understanding of itself as a community of principle and hence casts it in its best light. Were we to require instead that the judge decide the case only with a view to justice, we would have a truncated integrity, an integrity that failed to adhere to convictions of the fair distribution of political power and hence failed to capture all of the society's political and legal sense of who it is.

This part of Hercules's decision-making process in *McLoughlin* thus conforms in broad outline both to the hermeneutic picture of literary interpretation Dworkin sketches and to the hermeneutic approach to topics of justice we have attributed to Walzer and Rawls. Other aspects of the process seem odder in hermeneutic terms. Hercules begins his consideration of *McLoughlin* by setting out the six theories of legal rights that are "candidates for the best interpretation of the precedent cases" and he does so "even before he reads them."[20] Dworkin admits that these six theories constitute only a partial list of candidates for an interpretation of the precedents. Still, he argues that "Hercules chooses it ... because he knows that the principles captured in these interpretations have actually been discussed at length in the legal literature."[21] But why should he set out this partial list before he reads the cases and why should it matter which interpretive principles have been discussed in the legal literature? If Hercules's approach to the law is supposed to be interpretive, it would seem that he ought rather to begin by reading and trying to understand the relevant body of cases and precedents itself. In trying to continue a chain novel that consists in the beginning sections of Dickens's *A Christmas Carol*, we do not methodically run through the series of aesthetic principles captured in various interpretations of the book. Instead, we examine the particular themes, imagery and characters the book already possesses as thus far written; we try to determine the meaning they have as a unified whole and decide how they ought to be further developed given the meaning the book has when considered as the best example of its genre it can be. If interpretation and adjudication in the law are to follow the same process then it would seem that Hercules ought to begin not with the widely discussed interpretive principles of others but with the law as it has been articulated thus far, that he ought to try to determine the best meaning this law can be taken to have and further develop this meaning through his decision in the present case.

Dworkin might reply to this objection that the six principles Hercules selects for understanding the case-law relevant to *McLoughlin* already comprise the most plausible candidates and hence that Hercules is simply to start at a more sophisticated level than the one just sketched. He is to start with a list of interpretive possibilities that are already drawn from the history of the interpretation of the precedent cases and he is to ask which of these is to be accepted on the basis of considerations of fit and best light. Were we to accept this response, however, it would seem that Hercules ought to be interested to see which interpretive principle both fits the legal history and allows us to see it in the best light in which it can be seen given its relation to the other beliefs, practices and convictions of the society. Hercules, however, shortens his list by other means. Principle (1) is rejected for reasons of fit, but principles (2) and (3) are dismissed because, in Dworkin's view, they do not offer principled statements of rights at all.

From a strictly interpretive point of view, it is not clear why this circumstance should matter. The distinction between emotional injury suffered at the scene of an accident to a family member and emotional injury suffered later but because of the accident may not conform to what a given interpreter is used to considering as a principled statement of rights. The same might be said of considerations about community wealth. Still, it may be that either a temporal distinction or concerns about wealth not only fit the actual case history in question but might make of that history the best it can be. Hercules dismisses candidates (2) and (3) before he has even examined the case history on emotional injury. But if the task of the judge is the interpretive one on which Dworkin appears to insist, then it would seem precisely to involve examining this case history rather than deciding a priori what is or is not a principle of statement of rights.

Dworkin would likely reply that principled distinctions are part of law as integrity, that the idea that laws should make reasonable distinctions that can be justified with the same reasons we apply in other cases is part of what the enterprise of the law means. Conversely, to decide *McLoughlin* on the basis of either one of the interpretive candidates (2) or (3) would bring us too close to the kind of checkerboard solution law as integrity decisively rejects. But if this is the reason that Hercules dismisses interpretations (2) and (3), it seems that he might be moving too quickly. Suppose a temporal distinction between emotional injury suffered at the time and scene of an accident to a family member and emotional injury suffered later and elsewhere does fit the legal history. The interpretive judge's task would seem to be to see this distinction in its best light, to try to *find* some point in making such a distinction that is consistent with law as integrity. The approach Dworkin imagines for Hercules in deciding *McLoughlin v. O'Brian* seems, instead, to be close to the one he rejects in the aesthetic case. We are not supposed simply to impose our ideas of aesthetic value on a novel. Instead, while we may think any truly great novel must be a disquisition on the theme of death, we must also recognize that this feature may not reflect the best light in which to understand an Agatha Christie mystery. It is this novel, however, that we are to understand as the best *it* can be.

In other words, it would seem to follow from the example of the Agatha Christie novel that we try to find the way in which it is a good novel and that we therefore understand it as a mystery novel. Hence, it would seem that in the legal case we ought to try to find the way in which the principles embodied in the law according to our ideas of fit *can* be considered principles of law. Perhaps they ultimately cannot be. But we cannot come to this conclusion before we even read the cases; we must come to it rather by trying to understand the legal record itself and by trying to square it with other relevant law.

Dworkin's ambivalence with regard to this more immanent conception of the standards of fit and best light is also clear in his consideration of *Brown v. Board of Education*. Here he argues that because the Constitution deals with matters of fundamental importance, the judge cannot defer to popular morality. Moreover, because the Constitution is "foundational of other law," the terms in which a particular interpretation of its meaning are justified must themselves be "drawn from the most philosophical reaches of political theory."[22] Hercules thus composes a list of three accounts of a right against racial discrimination and asks which best articulates the principle behind the equal protection clause of the Fourteenth Amendment. The first account is a theory of suspect classifications under which there is no special right against racial discrimination; the right issues only from the more general right people have to be treated as equals according to whichever conception of equality their state holds. The second account is the theory of banned categories under which the right against discrimination is the right that certain properties such as race or sex not be used to distinguish groups of citizens for differential treatment. The third theory is the theory of banned sources. This theory first identifies the public interest with people's tastes and preferences and then claims that certain kinds of preferences are inadmissible in the calculation of this collective interest. The special right against racial discrimination issues, on this third theory, from the inadmissibility of racist preferences.

Hercules dismisses the first theory of suspect classifications on the grounds that it is unjust in principle and fails to fit the reasons Americans supported segregation in 1954. Either of the second two theories, however, lead to a decision in favor of the plaintiffs. As Dworkin writes,

Both fit the past pattern of Court decisions and the general structure of the Constitution well enough to be eligible. Both were consistent in 1954 with ethical attitudes that were widespread in the community; neither theory fits these attitudes noticeably better than the other because the difference between them appears only at a level of analysis popular opinion had not been forced to reach.[23]

But the same question arises here that arose in the case of *McLoughlin v. O'Brian*, namely, what is actually interpretive about this approach? Hercules does not try to understand the meaning of the equal protection clause directly in any of the ways he might have: by interpreting the meaning of the written text, by trying to understand the historical intentions of its framers, by trying to understand their complex meaning for segregated education in 1954 or by looking at the interpretive history of the equal protection clause developed in post-Civil War decisions from the *Slaughterhouse* cases through the civil rights cases. Instead, he examines a set of general accounts of the right against racial discrimination. These must fit the ethical attitudes of Americans in 1954; they must also fit "the past pattern of Court decisions and the general structure of the Constitution;" but they must fit them merely "well enough." One might claim that the ethical attitudes Americans held in 1954 are relevant to deciding *Brown* because law as integrity dictates that the court must include in its decision a recognition of the proper role of the judiciary and a respect for the claims of democracy. Still, it would seem that the task of deciding the case must remain that of understanding what the equal protection clause means for segregated education. We can insist that understanding this meaning also involves understanding how the Fourteenth Amendment is related to the American Constitution as a whole, to the proper domain of legal decision and to American ideals of liberty and equality in general. But it is still not clear why this insistence ought to turn our attention away from understanding the meaning of the equal protection clause itself or why it ought to involve inspecting the relative merits of theories of suspect classifications, banned categories and banned sources.

If the court's task is to determine the meaning of the equal protection clause, it would seem that, rather than looking at such general accounts, it ought to examine what meaning an equal protection of the laws has within the American framework of laws, norms and beliefs, what the legal history and experience means and, indeed, who Americans, as a people, take themselves to be. If we are to employ Dworkin's standards of fit and best light, then it would seem that the question is not which account of a right against racial discrimination fits the cases "well enough." It is rather which understanding of the meaning of the equal protection clause itself can both be integrated with the American Constitution and American norms and allow us to see that integration in the best light in which it can be seen. Despite Dworkin's hermeneutic language, his own concerns involve abstract principle. They are not what the American Constitution or a particular legal record means; they are rather what theory of equality or legal rights is the best and, in this regard, the Constitution and the legal record seem to offer only a kind of legal purchase on formal theory.

The dangers of this procedure can be documented by looking again at the decision in *Plessy v. Ferguson*, the decision that *Brown*, in effect, overturned. To the extent that Hercules appeals to existing theories of a right against racial discrimination he seems to make the same kind of appeal simply to existing principle that is made by the majority opinion in *Plessy*. On the one hand, the opinion states that "The object of the Amendment was undoubtedly to enforce the absolute equality of the two races before the law." On the other hand, it then quickly appeals to existing "truths" and claims that "in the nature of things [the amendment] could not have been intended to abolish distinctions based upon color."[24] This opinion might be regarded as a sincere attempt to interpret the Fourteenth Amendment but it remains imprisoned within the assumption of an immutable "nature of things." Indeed, even though Justice Harlan dissented from the opinion, he saw no reason to doubt either the superiority of the "white race" or its right to social ascendency. The white race is dominant, he writes, "in prestige, in achievement, in education, in wealth and in power. So I doubt not, it will continue to be for all time, if it remains true to its great heritage and holds fast to the principles of constitutional liberty."[25] In relying on existing accounts of a right against racial discrimination, Dworkin risks a similar myopia. He risks the same in the *McLoughlin* case in relying on what he simply takes to be the definition of a principled statement of rights. For Dworkin, as for the court in *Plessy v. Ferguson*, the constraints on interpretation seem ultimately not to be those of fit and best light, but those imposed on our understanding by the "truths" we already accept; it is to these that we are obliged to fit or misfit our texts.

In thus abandoning the idea of understanding a text or practice in terms of its own "fit" and "best light" and reverting to a more conventionistic mode of justification, Dworkin misses what is to be gained from a hermeneutic approach. As long as understanding a law, statute or part of the Constitution as the best that it can be requires finding a familiar conception of rights or equal treatment that a statute or part of the Constitution can be said to fit, we shall have to run through our existing conceptions until we find one that the legal record fits "well enough." But, if we take a more hermeneutic stance to the notions of "fit" and "best light," then understanding how a law is the most coherent and, indeed, the best it can be involves finding a perspective from which its own point is illuminated. This perspective has less to do with the nature of things than with an understanding of the law that is beholden to the situation within which we understand it and to our history and experience in general. Under this conception, our efforts to understand involve a process of education, for the perspective that turns out to be the most illuminative of the meaning of a law can be a new one for us, one that may not conform to theories we already possess. In asking the question of what the equal protection clause means for segregated education in 1954, for example, and in requiring the text of the clause to be coherent and the best it can be, we can discover new dimensions of the meaning both of the clause and of equality itself. We might develop the idea of equality to include equality of opportunity or we might rethink a distinction between social and political equality. The point here is that the particular interpretive perspectives we need to take to answer the particular questions that arise in the course of a society's development about its history, legal constitution and the like may teach us something; finding the perspective from which sense and, indeed, meaningfulness become clear may require that we refine, develop and change our existing philosophical and political theories to take account of new aspects of meaning. Conversely, to focus on the accounts of a right against racial discrimination that we already possess may be to miss the chance to revise these accounts and even to develop ourselves.

The same might be said about the principles Hercules uses to decide the *McLoughlin* case. Perhaps some of these principles ought ultimately to be rejected; nonetheless, if we dismiss them a priori, on the grounds of theories or ideas that we already accept, then we are prevented from questioning those theories and ideas themselves and prevented from learning from our material new ways of understanding the issues under study or the concepts we take for granted. A hermeneutic approach requires us to try to make sense out of our material. If we cannot, the fault may lie with us or with our own theoretical blinders. Taylor makes a similar point with regard to social scientific understanding. "In the sciences of man insofar as they are hermeneutical there can be a valid response to 'I don't understand' which takes the form, not only 'develop your intuitions', but more radically 'change yourself.' "[26]

This idea of learning from that which we are trying to understand obviously raises a problem, however, since it would seem
that different groups can learn different lessons from the texts and
text analogues they attempt to understand. Different people can
certainly learn different lessons from a piece of literature and can
learn different lessons at different times of their lives. Because of
our historically acquired sensitivity to the issue of anti-semitism,
the lesson we may learn from *The Merchant of Venice* may be a lesson not about Jews but about prejudice. Still, the play remains open
to alternative, less benign "teachings" and the same would seem to
hold of the lessons citizens can learn from both their history and
their laws. Why should the lessons of the Vietnam War necessarily
involve shunning imperialist ventures, for example, as opposed to
engaging in them with full military force and without monitoring
by news organizations? In fact, one might argue that the majority
opinion in *Plessy v. Ferguson* stemmed less from a reliance on
"nature" than from a simply racist reading of the Fourteenth
Amendment, a reading that allowed the Court to learn some way
in which the meaning of equality is compatible with the practice of
segregation and for which the appeal to "nature" was simply a
cover. Dworkin admits that in adjudicating cases in the law the
judge's "own moral and political convictions are directly engaged."[27] And elsewhere he concludes, "If my claims about the
role of politics in legal interpretation are sound, then we should expect to find distinctly liberal or radical or conservative opinions not
only about what the Constitution and laws of our nation should be
but also about what they are. And this is exactly what we do
find."[28] But what are we to do with this finding? What if the opinions we find are not simply liberal, radical and conservative, but
racist, sexist and fascist as well? Are these legitimate as long as
they are genuinely hermeneutic?

It is important to be clear as to what the problem that arises here
is. Certain interpretations of meaning may pass the tests of both fit
and best light. That is, they may be able to account for all the parts
of a text or text analogue and to show how they fit together to
form an internally consistent whole. Furthermore, they may be able
to show how the text or text analogue is the best it can be still, the
best for them may, as in the case of *Plessy v. Ferguson*, be racist or
otherwise objectionable. If this is the education received for our efforts to understand, it may be wondered what the hermeneutic enterprise has wrought. Can a hermeneutic approach to issues of
justice control the range of understanding? Are there not interpretations of meaning that comply with the standards of fit and best
light that are nonetheless despicable?

In order to pursue the issues raised by this possibility, I shall look briefly at Owen Fiss's account of the *Plessy* decision and of the constraints available to legal interpretation.

Objectivity and Correctness

For Fiss, the constraints that operate in any form of interpretation are certain "disciplining rules" which, for each domain of interpretation, specify a set of standards to which that kind of interpretation must adhere. Disciplining rules "specify the relevance and weight to be assigned to the material ... define basic concepts" and establish "the procedural circumstances under which the interpretation must occur."[29] Their importance lies in interpretation above the merely personal and subjective and in creating a kind of "professional grammar"[30] to which interpretations in a particular domain must conform. Disciplining rules are authoritative specifically for a particular interpretive community, Fiss argues, and, indeed, particular interpretive communities constitute themselves as professions by taking certain disciplining rules as authoritative for them. Interpretations that adhere to the rules of an interpretive community can be considered objective in just this sense, according to Fiss, in that they comply with the professional standards of that community. Such objectivity he calls a "bounded objectivity," the only kind of objectivity, he insists, "to which the law – or any interpretive activity – ever aspires and the only one about which we care."[31]

Disciplining rules do not completely eradicate what Fiss refers to as the creative role of the interpreter; nor does he think it is impossible that two equally constrained interpretations might differ from one another. Disciplining rules set the parameters within which interpretations can be legitimate, but they do not make a simply mechanical activity out of the process of understanding. Nor, according to Fiss, is every constrained interpretation "correct." In his view, both *Brown v. Board of Education* and *Plessy v. Ferguson* represent constrained interpretations because the court conformed to the proper professional rules in arriving at them and he concedes that to this extent, both are objective. Nonetheless, he insists that only *Brown* is correct and, moreover, that the incorrectness of *Plessy* can be shown on a variety of interpretive grounds. From an internal perspective, the decision can be criticized on the grounds that "the judges did not correctly understand the authoritative rules" or that they "misapplied them" or that they "failed to grasp the constitutional ideal of equality imported into the Constitution by the fourteenth amendment" or that they "incorrectly assumed that the affront to blacks entailed in the Jim Crow system was self-imposed."[32] From an external perspective, Fiss argues, the decision can be simply rejected as wrong on moral, political or religious grounds.

This distinction between constrained and correct interpretations appears to hold promise as a way of answering the problem we raised at the end of the last section. If is possible to adjudicate between different constrained interpretations then we no longer need worry about what we might learn from our efforts to understand. We can simply claim that the court learned well in deciding *Brown* and failed to learn at all in deciding *Plessy* because it misunderstood the disciplining rules or misapplied them. But take the claim that the majority opinion in *Plessy* can be shown to be simply incorrect because the judges did not correctly understand the disciplining rules. What can an incorrect understanding of the disciplining rules mean? Given Fiss's own distinction between constrained and correct interpretations, it cannot mean that it is unconstrained. But if it is constrained, on what basis is it wrong? Perhaps it is wrong for one of the other "internal" reasons that Fiss cites: namely, because the rules have been misapplied, because the judges "failed to grasp the constitutional ideal of equality imported into the Constitution by the fourteenth amendment" or because they "incorrectly assumed that the affront to blacks entailed in the Jim Crow system was self-imposed." These answers beg our question because each relies on an interpretation. Using any of them to reject the correctness of the opinion requires understanding the relevance of the disciplining rules, the ideal of equality or the affront to blacks in a particular way. But others may have different although equally constrained interpretations of all of these. Hence, the internal standard for designating any correct or incorrect remains unclear. If we want to argue that a particular interpretation of the ideal of equality is incorrect we can only appeal to our constrained reading of it and, as long as we rely solely on internal grounds, then it appears that we cannot escape the hermeneutic circle. Our understanding of which interpretations of the Constitution are incorrect will depend on our reading of the "evidence" and if our understanding is contested we can only, again, appeal to this reading.

Alternatively, we might adopt the external point of view and claim that the *Plessy* decision is wrong on moral, political or religious grounds. I claimed that this is Dworkin's ultimate strategy but it seems unsatisfying for two reasons. First, it seems to deny the possibility of learning from our material and even changing so that, for example, we can recognize new meanings the equal protection clause has. Second, the external point of view leaves the problem of a conflict of interpretations largely unresolved. If we are simply to pick between equally constrained interpretations on the basis of which seems for us to be correct given our moral, religious or political principles, there is, of course, no guarantee that we will all agree on moral, religious or political principles and, hence, no guarantee that we will find the same interpretations to be correct. Fiss contends that the virtue of American law is that it provides a hierarchy of authority for resolving such disputes. Hence, we need not be concerned that the interpretive community will come to blows over its differences because the Supreme Court is recognized as the final arbiter of all legal disputes. But even if we could attribute this same kind of hierarchy of authority to the domains of politics and literature, it is not clear how we can justify the correctness of the one interpretation made at the top. We shall see that for Alasdair MacIntyre legal adjudication in a liberal order, though methodical, is itself nonetheless arbitrary. In a reply to Fiss, Stanley Fish argues that a similar hierarchy does exist in the domain of literary studies, since the prestige and fame of some academics and academic institutions means that their interpretive commitments are taken more seriously than others. Still, in Fish's view, as in MacIntyre's, this circumstance indicates merely that what is at work in the resolution of both legal and literary disputes is less the rational constraint of disciplining rules than the assertion of irrational or at least arational power.[33]

Fish goes on to contend that because interpretation is a practice and because the understanding involved in a practice can never be formalized as a set of rules, Fiss's disciplining rules are simply superfluous. The game of basketball serves him as an example. Suppose a person has the skills of dribbling, shooting and so on required to play the game. Still, teaching him or her the actual game involves more than offering a set of disciplining rules such as "take only open shots" and "pass in certain circumstances" because no such set of rules will be inclusive enough to pertain to all the possible situations that might arise in a game. Instead the player has to grow into the game and come to understand it from the inside, as it were. This process is more a process of acquiring a "know-how" than one of knowing that one should pass if one is being guarded, for instance. We come to understand how to play a game rather than that we are to do such and such in circumstances thus and so. Interpretation, as well, according to Fish, is a practice we learn to do by doing it. The adequacy of our interpretations cannot be guaranteed through our abiding by certain learned and explicit rules any more than the adequacy of our basketball playing can. Fish writes:

> as the examples of the judge and the basketball player have shown, practice is already principled, since at every moment it is ordered by an understanding of what it is practice *of* (the law, basketball), an understanding that can always be put into the form of rules – rules that will be opaque to the outsider – but is not produced by them.[34]

Fish may have conceded more here than he seems to acknowledge. In claiming that our tacit understanding of how to do something can always be "put into the form of rules" he comes close to admitting Fiss's point: namely, that there are implicit rules within a practice that constrain its practitioners even if those practitioners do not themselves have an explicit knowledge of them. Moreover, Fiss insists, it is important that these rules be articulated since only such an articulation allows us to reflect upon the rationality or validity of the corresponding practice or action. That is, we can critically assess our practices and actions only if we can acquire an explicit knowledge of the rules and standards under which we are operating when we engage in them and to which we want them to comply.[35] Fiss suggests that it is because Fish denies the importance of such rules and standards that he must also identify all resolution of interpretive conflict with the assertion of power. For Fish, the kind of careful deliberation in which Hercules engages in deciding *Brown v. Board of Education* is no different in essence from packing the court. In each case, the task is to enforce one's own interpretation of the Constitution.

To a certain extent, the debate between Fiss and Fish over the role of disciplining rules mirrors the conflict we found internal to Dworkin's account of interpretation itself. On the one hand, just as Fish does, Dworkin wants to emphasize the political nature of interpretation. We differ in our interpretations of both case law and the American Constitution because we have different political views and different understandings of how the society involved is to be a community of integrity. The problem to which this analysis seems to lead, however, is that those differences may be so great that if we allow for them, we may also have to allow for racist, sexist or otherwise objectionable interpretations of meaning. On the other hand, then, just as Fiss does, Dworkin also wants to emphasize the constrained and, to this extent, rational character of interpretation. Interpretations are not political in any vulger sense but are, instead, disciplined by a set of professional standards that constrain the interpretations that can be taken seriously. In Dworkin's work, the standards that operate seem quickly to become abstractly moral and dogmatic ones, standards appropriate not to understanding meaning but to asserting philosophical truth. In Fiss's work, the standards are those of the American legal profession. But if the US Supreme Court is the final arbiter of legal disputes in the United States, does this mean its decisions are any more likely than even our own to satisfy the myriad ways in which Americans understand who they are? More importantly does it mean we can rely on their rationality?

In the next chapter I want to look at Jürgen Habermas's discourse ethics since it is directly concerned with the question of rationality and begins with a distinction similar to the one Fiss suggests between knowing how to engage in a practice and an explicit knowledge of the presuppositions of that practice. Indeed, Habermas suggests that to take a strictly interpretive approach to issues of justice is to invite cacophony. He does not suggest that we return to an external moral, religious or philosophical point of view however, to legislate dogmatically correct understanding. Rather, he argues that, through a collaboration of philosophy with "reconstructive" social sciences, we can uncover the universal pragmatic presuppositions of communication oriented towards understanding; moreover, the theoretically explicated knowledge of these pragmatic universals yields rational standards for adjudicating social conflicts.

5

HABERMAS AND THE CONFLICT OF INTERPRETATIONS

Whatever its virtues, the hermeneutic approach to questions of justice appears to raise difficulties that our excursion through the work of Walzer, Rawls and Dworkin seems to have only deepened. Walzer and Rawls require a kind of integrity from the ethical life of a society by insisting that its norms, ideals and practices complement one another in such a way as to compose a unified and coherent political culture. When certain practices, fundamental beliefs and social understandings deviate from others we have a basis for social criticism. Such criticism remains within a "hermeneutic circle" and simply holds up to the society a picture of what it could be that is based on an interpretation of its own shared meanings. Thus, rather than imposing an external and moralistic perspective, Walzer's and Rawls's versions of integrity require of the American society to which both belong that it understand what it is and live up to that self-understanding.

But this notion of integrity cannot itself resolve disputes over the best way to understand what American society is. We can emphasize different elements and dimensions of the beliefs and traditions of the societies to which we belong; we can also incorporate into these beliefs and traditions different inclusive pictures of our shared life and thereby produce different social and political understandings of who we are. Such differences are not resolved by Walzer's attempt to speak more clearly, if other interpreters are also speaking more clearly. Nor are they resolved by Rawls's identification of the best interpretation with that interpretation which can win the support of an overlapping consensus since we can have different ideas even of which concept of justice is workable or pragmatically justifiable in this way.

Consequently, we cannot dismiss the possibility that our actions, practices and convictions will be criticized from a perspective that is different from our own but equally internal and hermeneutic. The issue of the meaning of both medical care and the role of the United States in the war in Vietnam have served us as examples. If some Americans thought, with Rorty, that the war violated democratic principles of freedom and national self-determination, other Americans understood the meaning of these principles to require an even greater involvement on the part of the United States. We might call both interpretations of US actions "constrained" in Dworkin's sense in that they try to construct a coherent "text" out of American traditions, principles and practices and to make this text the best it can be by demanding of the United States that it be the best example that it can be of the kind of community it is meant to be. Nonetheless, these constraints do not rule out differences in the way Americans conceive of themselves as a society; nor do they provide a means of assuring the rationality of different lessons that might be learned from a society's texts and traditions. The Nazi interpretation of German history is perhaps the easiest example here. Although Dworkin, himself, does not seem to understand his constraints in this way, we might claim that their merit lies in promotion of a kind of education. By conceiving of the standards of fit and best light hermeneutically we can see our interpretive task as that of making sense out of and learning from that which we are trying to understand. But precisely this attempt to learn leaves us vulnerable. Suppose we learn from texts or text analogues in a way that degrades rather than educates us? Suppose what we gain from the hermeneutic enterprise is a racist and sexist education? Can hermeneutics itself provide any standards more definitive than fit and best light for adjudicating the rationality of a given interpretation?

From a Habermasian point of view just this sort of question indicates the need both for a less hermeneutic starting point and for a return to Kantian moral theory. Indeed, he suggests that the problem with Rawls's analysis in *A Theory of Justice* is not the universalism and proceduralism that his critics found and attacked in it. The problem is, rather, to find a way of justifying these characteristics in the proper way, and this Habermas tries to do in his "discourse ethics." I want first to discuss the differences between Habermas's and Rawls's reformulations of Kant's moral point of view and then to turn to a set of difficulties that seems to issue from Habermas's conception, at least with regard to the problem of rationally resolving interpretive conflicts in the way a society understands itself.

Habermas's Discourse Ethics

Habermas's "discourse ethics" is meant to follow from the articulation of a know-how into a know-that, from a reconstruction of the pre-theoretical knowledge participants in understanding themselves have of how to come to an understanding with one another. Habermas argues that competent speakers can themselves tell the difference between attempting to influence others causally and coming to an understanding with them over a course of action, normative principle, fact in the world or the like.[1] In the first case, the attempt is to secure a hearer's cooperation by whatever means possible and may therefore include deceit, coercion and manipulation. In the second case the speaker has to rely on the possibility of giving reasons for his or her claim or proposal. That is, a speaker secures the assent of a hearer to what Habermas calls a "speech act offer" by taking on the responsibility of giving grounds for his or her claim if it is challenged. "That a speaker can rationally motivate a hearer to accept such an offer is explained not by the validity of what is said but by the guarantee ... which the speaker takes over to try to redeem the ... claim if necessary."[2] Thus, whereas what Habermas calls strategic action has its basis in force, communicative actions are based on the possibility of offering acceptable reasons for the validity claims one makes.

Moreover, Habermas claims, an orientation to reaching understanding is the "original mode of language use" upon which other modes such as intentional deceit and manipulation are "parasitic."[3] Although the initial basis for this claim lay in Austin's distinction between illocutionary and perlocutionary acts, Habermas has since revised his account of perlocutionary effects to distinguish between those that lie in the domain of communicative action and those that follow from strategic goals. His basic point remains the same. The success of strategic uses of language depends upon their taking a communicative form. "The actor can accomplish his strategic goal ... only if he produces an illocutionary effect. Furthermore, he is successful only if the speaker pretends to pursue the illocutionary goal of his speech act without reservation and thereby leaves the hearer unclear as to the actually present one-sided infraction of the presuppositions of action oriented towards understanding."[4] The success of a lie, then, requires the hearer to accept the speech act offer as genuine, that is, as a claim that the speaker would be willing and able to defend if asked.

Habermas distinguishes three different spheres within which challenges to the claims involved in a speech act offer can be raised and may need to be redeemed. A hearer can challenge a speaker to show the sincerity of the offer or, in other words, that the speaker is accurately representing his or her intentions. In this case, the validity claim under dispute pertains to the speaker's inner world and the redemption of the validity claim is accomplished most adequately through action; the speaker acts in accordance with the intentions he or she has expressed and thereby proves the truthfulness of his or her expression of intention. But hearers can also challenge speakers to show the truth of the existential judgments contained in their claims or to show the rightness of their actions or of the norms of action they propose. In the first case of existential judgments the claim is related to the external world of facts and, in the second case of actions and norms of action, to the intersubjective world that speaker and hearer share. In both instances the redemption of the validity claim at issue is a discursive one. Speakers show the truth of their existential judgments or the rightness of their actions and norms of action by giving reasons for them that a hearer can accept.

At this point in his argument, Habermas follows Stephen Toulmin in contending that this discursive justification is part of an informal, as opposed to a formal, logic of argumentation. A rationally motivated agreement over the rightness of a norm or truth of a claim cannot be limited either to "deductively conclusive arguments" or to "empirically compelling evidence." The former are restricted to logical inferences and cannot motivate the rational agreement of a hearer on any matter that is not already contained in the premises of the argument. The latter rest on substantive contents and since, as we have seen, these may be interpreted in various different ways, they may not compel the assent of the hearer at all.[5] What then is the condition of well-grounded or rational assent and agreement?

Habermas's answer introduces the well-noted, if not well-understood, conception of an ideal speech situation. In attempting to reach an agreement over a disputed proposition or norm of action, participants to the discussion must make certain pragmatic presuppositions about the structure of the communication itself and these, Habermas argues, have a normative content. The participants must suppose that this structure excludes all constraints that might distort its conclusions such as the threat of sanctions, an inequality in the distribution of power within the communication, fears on the part of one or more participants or outright force. They must suppose that all participants to the discussion are motivated only by the concern to come to an agreement over truth or rightness and they must suppose that they can be persuaded by argument. In other words, they must suppose that, "in principle, all those affected participate as free and equal members in a cooperative search for truth in which only the force of the better argument may hold sway"[6]

These pragmatic presuppositions can obviously be counterfactual. Any actual agreement we reach with others over claims to the truth of propositions or the rightness of social norms may usually, in fact, reflect the force of unequal power relations, constraints of fear or strategic communications of one kind or another. Still, the consequence of denying the universal pragmatic presuppositions is what, following Karl-Otto Apel, Habermas calls a performative contradiction. If one were to argue that communication oriented to understanding does not have this pragmatic structure, one would nonetheless have to rely on it in making one's claim. That is, one would have to suppose that the communication which reached the conclusion that argumentation does not have this pragmatic structure itself did have this pragmatic structure, that the conclusion could be reached by a communication community of free and equal participants engaged in a cooperative search for truth and motivated only by the force of the better argument. Therefore, anyone who seriously participates in argumentation, Habermas thinks, implicitly accepts general pragmatic presuppositions that anticipate an ideal speech situation.

Formulated specifically as the principle of what Habermas calls a "discourse" or "communicative ethics" (*Diskursethik*), this general pragmatic situation means that "only those norms may claim to be valid which could meet with the assent of all concerned in their role as participants in a practical discourse" or argumentation.[7] In other words, valid norms of action are those all concerned could conclude to be valid were they to participate freely and equally in a cooperative effort to determine the validity of the norm in which only the force of the better argument held sway. Hence, Habermas specifies certain symmetry conditions – participants must have the same chances to contribute to the discourse, to make assertions, recommendations and explanations, to challenge claims and proposed justifications and to express feelings, wishes and needs[8] – and he introduces a modified Kantian principle of universalization, or "U" as a procedure of moral-practical discourse: "For a norm to be valid, the consequences and side-effects its general observance has for the satisfaction of each's particular interests must be freely acceptable to all."[9]

How does this proceduralist approach to the justification of moral and political norms compare to the Rawlsian one? According to Habermas, it opens out what he considers to be the monological character of Rawls's method. For Rawls, as we saw, the impartial point of view that parties to the original position adopt is written into the original position. Parties to it are symmetrically situated in identical conditions of ignorance; they choose principles of justice in accordance with their highest- and higher-order interests in developing and exercising their moral powers and in pursuing some determinate conception of the good. Since, however, they do not know what their socioeconomic positions or determinate conceptions of the good are, each person chooses principles of justice designed to be favorable to any conception of the good, any socioeconomic position and any talent or ability. Choice in the original position is unanimous and fair, then, not through discourse and deliberation among the parties and not because the parties are themselves accorded moral insight; it is unanimous and fair, rather, because each chooses principles of justice designed to preserve himself or herself from the worst-case scenario of living under principles of justice prejudiced against his or her position, abilities and conception of the good. "Each," Rawls writes "is forced to choose for everyone."[10]

In contrast, Habermas applauds Thomas Scanlon's revised version of "contractualism," one that begins with "ordinary forms of moral reasoning."[11] It is characteristic of these forms for Scanlon, as for Habermas, that the individuals engaged in them are themselves motivated by "the desire to be able to justify [their] actions to others on grounds they could not reasonably reject."[12] Whereas Rawls's principles of justice articulate "what it would be rational for a self-interested person to choose or agree to under the assumption of ignorance or equal probability of being anyone," Scanlon appeals to the "idea of what it would be unreasonable for people to reject given that they are seeking a basis for general agreement."[13] We now begin not with parties behind a veil of ignorance who choose in silent isolation from all other parties to the original position; we begin rather with ordinary individuals who are credited with a concern to justify their actions and norms of action to others and who are already seeking a basis for general agreement. This situation means that it is no longer enough for each individual to decide alone which principles of justice he or she can approve as favorable to himself or herself; parties to Scanlon's contract must instead consider the question of what everyone could reasonably approve of or what no one could reasonably reject. This requires understanding not merely what it would be rational for oneself to accept or reject but what it would be rational for others, who one knows are not in the same situation as oneself, to accept or reject.

Scanlon admits that in making this assessment the idea of the original position or, in general, the idea of putting oneself in another's place may be a "useful corrective device."[14] The attempt to justify principles of justice through recourse to the idea of a social contract must face the problem that the parties to the contract can easily take a given proposed principle's advantages to themselves more seriously than its forseeable costs to others. In order to avoid this possibility, any social contract theory must be combined with a more Kantian perspective and Scanlon concedes that the idea of imaginatively putting oneself behind a veil of ignorance represents one possible strategy. At the same time, he insists that the purpose of the device must remain that of simply providing a way for theorists to consider what *all* could judge to be capable of universal approval.

In this regard Habermas goes further than Scanlon. On his account, the idea of putting oneself in another's place, whether one uses the image of a veil of ignorance or some other device, cannot be conceived of simply as an instrument for correcting a contractual model of moral reasoning. Instead, it points to a different model of moral reasoning altogether: namely, that of discourse. If we take as our starting point moral-practical argumentations in which we are concerned to reach agreement with others over a disputed action or norm of action, then it becomes clear that we always are already constrained to put ourselves in another's place, that the procedure of "ideal role-taking" is already part of the structure of our discourse insofar as we are engaged in a cooperative search for truth and insofar as only the force of the better argument may hold sway.

As against Rawls's recourse to the original position, then, and in accord with Scanlon's version of contractualism, Habermas considers the mark of a justified principle "what all can will in agreement to be a universal norm."[15] A discourse ethics does not try to determine what each individual would choose under universalizing conditions as the best solution for himself or herself to a choice problematic; it begins, in contrast, with the idea of a rational consensus. As against Scanlon's account, however, Habermas claims that the appropriate model for this idea is not that of a contract at all, even one to which corrective, Kant-inspired thought-experiments have been added in order to assure its fairness. The appropriate model is, instead, that of discursive justification. As he writes, "Practical discourse can be understood as a process of reaching agreement which, through its force, that is solely on the basis of unavoidable general presuppositions of argumentation, constrains all participants at the same time to ideal role-taking."[16]

Rawls's failure to move from a social contract theory to discourse is not the only defect Habermas finds in Rawls's conception of the procedure of choice in the original position. He argues that Rawls must also confront the problem of relating his theory of justice to the moral-practical life a society already possesses. Representatives to the original position are to choose in a rationally autonomous way while the structure of the original position is to make this rational choice both unanimous and fair. But if these representatives are thus themselves deprived of moral insight, Habermas insists that it also becomes unclear why they would consent to the conditions of the original position in the first place or why they would abide by the choice made under those conditions once the veil of ignorance were lifted.[17] The problem here is obviously similar to the one Rawls's hermeneutically oriented critics raise to *A Theory of Justice*. If we must imagine conditions for grounding principles of justice that are not the conditions under which we live, what possible relevance can either these grounds or the principles they legitimate have for us?

Of course, Rawls's recent work tries to clarify his response to this problem by basing the choice of principles of justice on model conceptions drawn from the practical and political life democratic societies already have. Individuals do not need to be motivated to assent to the conditions of the original position or to the results of choice under them; rather these conditions and their results are based on an interpretation of the political beliefs and public traditions they already share. But we have seen that just this response raises the problem of justification in a different way. As members of a democratic political culture, we now have to show that the original position marks a pragmatically feasible interpretation of what we regard as fair conditions and that the idea of moral persons presents a workable picture of what freedom and equality mean to us.

It is in this regard that Habermas's discourse ethics seems to provide a better option. It does not locate the grounds for normative principles in an original position that is constructed by the moral theorist in the hope of thereby establishing an overlapping consensus. It locates the grounds of normative principles in the pragmatic presuppositions ordinary individuals themselves always already make in entering into argumentations with others. Nor are these presuppositions meant to be fictions created by the theorist in an effort to picture our shared social meanings in a way we can all find reasonable. Habermas claims that they represent the results of a reconstructive science or, in other words, that they can be shown to reflect the pre-theoretical knowledge of speakers and actors of how to come to a rationality based agreement with others. Hence the account of practical discourse has an empirical basis in ordinary discourses.

Still this is an empirical basis with a difference. Rawls can close the gap between the original position and the actual ethical world we inhabit only by claiming that the original position is a way of articulating the normative principles of this world and that the two principles of justice that issue from it can be supported by an over-lapping consensus. A discourse ethics is meant to be embedded in the pragmatic structure of communicative understanding rather than the content of particular traditions; importantly, it thereby seems to remain independent of the substantive norms and beliefs a society already possesses and independent of the different ways it can interpret them. A discourse ethic does not rely on claims about what we believe but rather depends on more formal or for-mal-pragmatic features of our communication. In this way it also seems to provide an independent standpoint for a critical assess-ment of norms and beliefs. These two possibilities of avoiding in-terpretive difficulties and providing critical standards are the ones I want to explore in the rest of this chapter.

The Problem of Interpretation

A discourse ethics does not involve the formulation of new norms or principles of action; instead it concerns only the justification of disputed norms which are brought to the test that a discourse ethics establishes from out of the "life-world" of concrete social practices and actions. For purposes of justifying norms the prag-matic presuppositions of argumentation require that we look to the assent of participants in an ideal speech situation. But from the idea that only those norms are valid which could meet with the assent of all concerned as free and equal participants in a practical dis-course we, as moral theorists, can derive no actual specific norms. Habermas therefore defends a rigorously Kantian position: "Funda-mental norms of justice and morality are not the responsibility of moral theory; they must be considered as the contents that require grounding in practical discourse."[18] And as he writes in "Moralität und Sittlichkeit" (Morality and Ethical Life), "The content that is tested in light of a moral principle is produced not by the philoso-pher but by real life."[19]

From this perspective, Rawls's procedure in depriving social agents themselves of moral insight is doubly problematic. The moral theorist not only contrives the universalizing conditions that make a rational choice of principles conform to the "reasonable" conditions of fair social cooperation; the moral theorist also figures out which principles they would choose under these conditions. But we thereby confront the problem not only of justifying the initial conditions under which the agents are to choose principles of justice. We also have to show that the principles the theorists think they would choose are the best solution to the choice problematic given the other options. Some of Rawls's critics have been unconvinced by his proof.[20] Habermas, for his part, places the responsibility for determining and testing normative principles on the participants in practical discourses themselves. The standpoint of moral and political theory must be a wholly critical one that cannot take the place of collective decision-making by social actors themselves. The principle of universalization tells us not what our norms and principles must be, but under what conditions they would have to be assented to in order to be legitimate.

Still, as formulated by a discourse ethics, are these conditions not so strict that, in practice anyway, no norms could possibly pass the discursive test? "U" or the principle of universalization states that "for a norm to be valid, the consequences and side effects its general observance has for the satisfaction of each's particular interests must be freely acceptable to all." This formulation of the principle differs from Kant's both in its consideration of consequences and side effects and in its concern for the interests of all those affected. According to Habermas, the attention to consequences allows a discourse ethics to avoid the charge of "abstract universalism" that Hegel attributes to Kant. A discourse ethics is not insensitive to the results of action but brings consideration of them directly into the argumentation.[21] Similarly, the attention to the interests of all those affected allows a discourse ethics to avoid certain dichotomies Hegel criticizes in Kant's ethics. The concern of a discourse ethics is not primarily the determination of one's duty against inclination; nor does it set reason against interest. Its concern is rather to determine whether all affected could agree to a norm given each of their specific circumstances and interests. Hence, according to the discourse ethics, we are to suppose the general observance of a proposed norm, cash out the forseeable consequences and side effects of this state of affairs for each person's particular interests and ask whether all of us affected could freely accept them.

Once we focus on consequences, circumstances and interests, however, it is not clear that we can ever agree on which interests are generalizable in this way unless we already share interests and circumstances. Take a norm of action that sanctions the infliction of unnecessary suffering.[22] Its general observance seems to work against the satisfaction of the interests of some of those concerned, namely those who would suffer injury through it, and they might therefore not accept it freely. If we reverse the norm under consideration to one that prohibits the infliction of unnecessary suffering because such infliction cannot be freely assented to by all, still others among us might not freely accept the consequences and side effects of this second proposed norm's general observance. If we are masochists we will want to suffer some intentional harm by some others and the norm prohibiting such behavior will be seen as a violation of our interests and private conception of the good. We might change the norm, again, to one prohibiting the infliction of unnecessary suffering unless it is freely consented to by those who would suffer. Yet, some might argue that occurrences of even consensual suffering affect their interests detrimentally since they encourage an environment of violence and of what they consider sexual perversion. What norms in fact could we all freely assent to as members of a modern pluralistic society in which we have developed different and competing interests as well as different and competing values and conceptions of the good?

It might be argued that the example of unnecessary suffering is too extreme to prove any point since it turns on a recognized oddity, namely, the possible existence of masochistic interests. Indeed, we could argue that masochistic interests are not only odd but perverse. Hence, before we can entertain them in a discourse freed of all external and internal constraints, we need a theory to help us discover the childhood experiences that might have given rise to them. But we have other normative disagreements that do not turn on recognized oddities. Suppose we examine the legitimacy according to the discourse ethics of a social norm that sanctions, among other actions and practices, segregated schooling for blacks and whites. If we focus on the interests of those involved, we might say that its general observance works against the satisfaction of the interests of those of us who would benefit from being educated in an integrated setting, whether because we would be better educated or because we could go to a school closer to our home. Hence, it is arguable that norms supporting racial segregation would clearly not allow for the assent of all in an ideal speech situation.

Suppose we reverse the norm to one that prohibits segregated public schools and other discriminatory social practices. In this case, we seem to risk the dissent of those whose interests have the opposite thrust. We might claim that these interests cannot be supported with good reasons and, hence, the claims connected to them cannot withstand challenge in an unconstrained practical discourse. But there also might be objections to the norm and to the assumption of the generalizability of the interests at its base that are not overtly racist and can even be supported with what to some, anyway, might appear to be good reasons. A case in point might be Hannah Arendt's 1959 argument against school desegregation on the basis of an Aristotelian distinction between the social and the political. Arendt argued that within the social sphere, as opposed to the political sphere, discrimination was outside the domain of governmental regulation and that because education encompassed the social right of individuals to associate only with those with whom they wanted to associate, enforcing school integration was a mistake. She also claimed that in placing black children at the forefront of the fight, the advocates of school desegregation violated another (generalizable) norm: namely, that of not requiring a defenseless group to suffer the consequences of the beliefs of others.[23]

Perhaps Arendt had motives in making this argument other than a concern for the truth or normative rightness. Perhaps, in any case, she might have been persuaded by the better arguments of others. Conversely, it may be that the assumptions, values and notions of the good life which lie behind Arendt's argument are so different from those motivating the *Brown v. Board of Education* decision that any of hope of a rational consensus over norms is not only utopian but fundamentally misconceived. Habermas has two responses to observations of this kind. First, he argues that "as interests and value orientations become more differentiated in modern societies, the morally justified norms that control the individual's scope of action in the interest of the whole become ever more general and abstract."[24] Second, he concedes that in cases in which it is impossible to agree on a generalizable interest compromise may become necessary to regulate irreconcilable particular interests. But he adds the proviso that "fair compromise in turn calls for morally justified procedures of compromising."[25] I want to examine this second position and then return to the first.

With the idea of "morally justified procedures of compromising" Habermas appeals to the normative content of the pragmatic structure of practical argumentation. Morally justified procedures are those to which everyone concerned could agree as free and equal participants in a practical discourse. The problem that seems to lead to the necessity of compromise is that the universalistic conditions of practical discourse are too strict to allow us to accept the legitimacy of either the proposed norm, its opposite or some inventive combination of some parts of each. If this is the case, however, can the conditions of practical discourse not also be too strict to achieve agreement on morally justified procedures for compromising? If our conceptions of our interests differ as radically as they seem or seemed to do in the case of school desegregation, cannot similar differences undermine any attempt to reach a consensus on morally justified procedures for reaching a compromise? Given the differences in the values and assumptions behind Arendt's argument against school desegregation, on the one hand, and behind more liberal arguments for school desegregation, on the other, is it not likely that similar differences will enter into attempts to find legitimate standards for compromising as well?

Habermas makes it clear that what serves as the criterion for a justified norm of action in practice is not as much the universal assent of an ideal communication community as, instead, the assumption that the rules of argumentation that discourse participants must presuppose are adequately realized for the purposes at hand. There are certain rules of argumentation that participants must follow if they are to engage in argument at all. They must formulate their claims in intelligible ways, exchange validity claims and so on. But with regard to the idealized conditions of discourse they need only assume a realization commensurate with the goal of the specific argumentation:

> Discourses occur under the limitations of space and time and within social contexts; participants in argumentation are not intelligible characters and are also moved by motives other than the only one allowed by the cooperative search for truth; themes and contributions must be ordered, the beginning, end and recommencement of discussions regulated, relevance secured and competence assessed. Because all of this is the case, institutional measures are required which can neutralize unavoidable empirical limitations and avoidable external and internal influences to the extent that the idealized conditions presupposed can be fulfilled at least in sufficient approximation.[26]

But this clarification still raises a problem of interpretation, for it is not clear that we can always agree on what sufficient approximation means in a particular case. That which serves to legitimate a norm of action, principle or, indeed, procedure of compromise is the assent of all concerned in a discourse which sufficiently approximates the idealizing assumptions we necessarily make in argumentation with one another. The question of whether a given norm does meet these conditions cannot be answered speculatively. We need actually to engage in a discourse that sufficiently approximates ideal conditions and hence we need to take certain measures to ensure an adequate exclusion of distorting conditions. But we can surely have different ideas of what, in any given case, constitutes both a sufficient approximation to ideal conditions and an adequate exclusion of distorting factors. We must therefore forge a consensus on what both mean before we engage in a practical discourse over norms but if this prior consensus is to be legitimate, it must already itself approximate ideal conditions.

We seem to move in a circle. If, in our attempts to determine fair procedures of compromise, we begin with different notions of what counts as a sufficient approximation to an ideal speech situation, we shall need to come to an initial agreement about the elements of such a sufficient approximation. But if this initial agreement is itself to be legitimate it must itself be acceptable to all under conditions that already sufficiently approximate an ideal speech situation. We can perhaps conclude that we must therefore begin in the middle, with vague ideas and agreements that we then concretize and develop in the course of our discussion. But, in order for such concretization and development themselves to be legitimate, it would seem that their conditions must also be those of an ideal speech situation. Otherwise, how will we know or agree that various distorting factors such as those of power, wealth or intimidation have been sufficiently neutralized not only in our final compromise but in the process by which we come to it?

Any compromise must be fair and, from the point of view of a discourse ethics, this means that the procedure through which it is reached must reflect a consensus reached under a sufficient approximation to the conditions of practical discourse. But we may turn out to have not only competing interests but different interpretations of what counts as a sufficient approximation to ideal conditions in a given instance. What about Habermas's first reply to disagreement: namely, that in modern pluralistic societies "the morally justified norms that control the individual's scope of action in the interest of the whole become ever more general and abstract"? Here we might ask, first, whether these norms are not so general and abstract that they become inadequate to deal with the controversies that arise in such societies over the concrete questions of justice and action. Second, if dealing with these concrete questions, therefore, involves supplying some more concrete content to the general norms, does this content not raise problems of interpretation that are similar to those we considered in the case of a consensus on norms of compromise? Doing justice to Habermas's treatment of the issues involved here requires exploring the distinction he makes between practical discourse, on the one hand, and forms of therapeutic and aesthetic discussion, on the other.

Habermas insists that any procedural ethics from Kant's through Rawls's and including a discourse ethics must distinguish "normative statements about the hypothetical 'justice' of actions and of norms from evaluative statements about subjective preferences."[27] Elsewhere Habermas includes under "evaluative expressions" a person's or group's interpretations of its desires, feelings, and needs (*Bedürfnisnatur*).[28] These are tied to one's identity and cultural heritage and bound up with specific notions of the good. Hence they do not lend themselves to a consensus that is meant to be universally binding and in *The Theory of Communicative Action* Habermas therefore distinguishes practical discourse from both aesthetic criticism and therapeutic critique. The function of aesthetic criticism is to assess "the vocabulary of our evaluative language generally;"[29] that of therapeutic critique to clarify for patients their own self-deceptions about their needs and desires.

Neither form of argumentation can conform to the standards of practical discourse or duplicate its scope. The function of aesthetic criticism is to bring others to see a work of art or performance in the way we see it and to accept the standards of value we claim it embodies. But our claims about the work or standards of value cannot be directly justified with reasons. We can refer to the emotions and desires that the work may elicit from us; we can point to phenomena of color, form and so on and appeal to what we hope are our audience's evaluative sensibilities. But these emotions, perceptions and appeals to a sensibility do not of themselves validate either our idea of the work of art in particular or our standards of value in general. They are meant rather to guide the emotions, perceptions and sensibilities of our audience and to encourage or allow its members to have the same experience of the work and value standards that we have. Nor does our audience's failure to have the emotions, perceptions and sensibilities we want it to have indicate necessarily either that it is irrational or that we are. The validity of a normative claim, for Habermas, depends upon the possible assent of a universal audience as free and equal participants in a practical discourse. But, in discussions of art or value standards, justification is less global. As he writes, "The circle of intersubjective recognition that forms around cultural values does not yet in any way imply a claim that they would meet with general assent within a culture, not to mention universal assent."[30]

Similarly, with regard to therapeutic critique "important presuppositions for discourse in the strict sense are not fulfilled."[31] At least some of the patient's claims are not taken as validity claims and examined for their truth or rightness but are rather regarded as symptoms of an underlying pathology. Patient and therapist are thus not meant to be free and equal dialogue partners; rather, the patient is partially objectified: his or her validity claims are not to be understood as claims or tested discursively; they are rather explained as the causal results or symptoms of early childhood events. Nor does only the force of the better argument hold sway in the therapeutic situation. Of equal or greater power are the situation of transference, the emotions it awakens, the catharsis the patient may experience and so on. The goal is not a justification of the patient's needs and desires as ones to the validity of which all can assent as participants in discourse; what matters ultimately is simply what patients become capable of either accepting or revising about themselves.[32]

Given this distinction between practical discourse, on the one hand, and forms of aesthetic and therapeutic discussion, on the other, we might argue that where we can together settle on no generalizable interest, as in the case in which different interests seem to undermine a consensus on norms against unnecessary suffering, we need to engage in a different kind of discussion, a discussion, namely, of our interpretations of our needs and desires. This sort of conversation bears no universalistic implications but rather signals the sharp divide between a rational agreement over norms and a contingent agreement in values. We can hope for consensus on abstract and general norms, then because their abstractness and generality ensure that they will be indifferent to differences in our values and conceptions of the good. And where differences in our values and conceptions of the good do matter, we can pursue a different kind of discussion, at least initially, a discussion oriented to granting us better access to our real needs and interests.

Still, even if we reserve notions of rational agreement for abstract and general norms and leave discussion of values to more intimate circles, we must ultimately also determine the meaning of norms for particular issues. This attempt seems simply again to have to confront differences in interpretation and evaluation. Habermas cites universal human rights as examples of norms of action that can be justified according to the conditions of practical discourse.[33] But what exactly are these rights? While we in the West at least, might all agree on a right to free speech, it is notorious that we can disagree on what counts as speech and hence on what actions are supposed to fall under the right to it. Rights to life and liberty have also been very differently interpreted in disputes over the morality of abortion. The normative questions in this case seem to include questions of whether the right to life includes a fetus's right to life and what the scope and meaning of a woman's liberty or rights over her body are. Answers to these questions seem to depend on how we interpret the meaning of life and liberty and these interpretations, in turn, seem to depend, not on the arguments and reasons that we appeal to in practical discourse, but on our cultural values and religious upbringing.

The question of values, interpretations and sensibilities thus appears to extend beyond the question of an individual's or group's perversions and self-deceptions and beyond the scope of purely aesthetic issues to enter the moral-practical domain itself. We cannot come to a consensus on what the right to privacy means concretely because we disagree in our interpretations of the meaning of the terms involved in the articulation of the right and in our judgment of the relevant matters. Nor can we be simply argued out of these evaluations and interpretations for the different assumptions and value orientations at the base of the different positions set different terms for what each side can consider valid argumentation. But, if this is the case, then the sanctity of the moral domain as a sphere of debate susceptible to universal consensus seems to be threatened. To the extent that our claims about the concrete meaning of a general and abstract norm depend upon evaluations and interpretations that are bound up with our cultural heritage, religious traditions and conceptions of the good, the circle of intersubjective recognition that forms around it would seem to be as restricted in practical argumentation as in forms of therapeutic and aesthetic discussion. We can hope for agreement, it seems, only with those whose values and interpretations overlap ours to a sufficient extent, as "hermeneuticists" such as Williams and Rorty have already claimed. Elsewhere, we may have to contend not just with disagreements that we can attribute to the personal irrationality of those with whom we are speaking; we shall also have to recognize the possibility of moral-practical dissensus based simply on interpretive and evaluative differences.

The problem here might be regarded as strictly a problem of application. The assent of all under ideal conditions is meant to serve as the criterion for the validity of norms of action, however, and Habermas does not argue that such norms contain prescriptions for their own application. Under this analysis, if the principle of privacy rights is legitimate it is because all concerned could assent to it as free and equal participants in a practical discourse; the question of whether the principle can be applied to the issue of abortion remains a separate question.[34] Habermas does not think such questions can be resolved by a neo-Aristotelian appeal to a moral agent's sensibilities, *phronesis* and capacities for judgment.

The moral point of view requires not only the impartial justification of a norm but its impartial application. "In this dimension," he claims "completely uncontemptible *topoi* are valid: for instance, the principles that all relevant aspects of a case must be considered ... and that means should be proportionate to ends."[35]

It is difficult to see, however, either how the domain of application is to be thereby freed from the problem of interpretive and evaluative differences or, indeed, how the question of applying a norm can be distinguished from the question of its meaning. When we have to determine the meaning of a particular right, it would seem that we need to know what particular disputes or what kind of dispute it is supposed to adjudicate as well as how it might adjudicate them. We cannot determine what the right to free speech means unless we have some idea of what its domain of application is, that is, unless we understand what kinds of issues might be free speech issues, what kinds of actions clearly count for the society in question as speech and about what kinds of actions the society is still unclear with regard to their status as speech. To this extent, even our understanding of an abstract and general norm must include some concrete content and hence some applicatory force. Otherwise it is not clear how we could understand it as anything at all.[36] Nor is it clear how we could posit a consensus over the meaning of a right while also conceding that we might disagree on how to apply it. In fact, in discussing issues of application, Habermas does not consider the question of how the meaning of a general human right is itself to be determined. He is concerned only with the issue of how we are to apply a norm, which he takes to have already been defined, to a new instance or problem. Yet, when we disagree on the domain of application of a norm such as the right to free speech or the right to privacy, it remains unclear how normative discourse on the right itself can comply with the universalistic conditions Habermas requires for it.

Moreover, were we to understand an issue such as whether abortion can be morally justified as a problem strictly of applying a previously defined and agreed upon right, it would appear that this application still includes interpretive questions. At issue here are the *topoi* that Habermas introduces according to which we are to consider all relevant aspects of a case and to find means that are appropriate to our ends. Surely, when we consider all relevant aspects of a case, we can differ in our assessments of which aspects are relevant because we differ in how we interpret and evaluate the matters under study. By the same token, if means must be proportionate to ends, the question of which means in a given case are proportionate to the ends in question remains itself an interpretive and evaluative question. If we understand the meaning of a right to life to cover the life of a fetus, then certain means such as bombing abortion clinics may seem perfectly appropriate even if it involves risking the life of "murderous" doctors and pregnant women. How practical discourse can rise above these different assessments and how the application of consensual norms might avoid the problems they seem to raise remains unclear.

One of Habermas's responses to such a conclusion seems to be to subject our interpretations and evaluations themselves to the conditions of practical discourse. Despite his recognition of legitimate differences in value standards, he also argues that idiosyncratic evaluations, or evaluations that fail to meet wider community standards, are irrational unless they have the "innovative" character of art.[37] And despite the difference he establishes between practical discourse, on the one hand, and forms of aesthetic and therapeutic discussion, on the other, he also argues that "even the interpretations in which the individual identifies the needs that are most peculiarly his own are open to a revision process in which *all* participate."[38] The same claim is made at more length in *Legitimation Crisis*:

> Since all affected have, in principle, at least the chance to participate in practical deliberation, the "rationality" of the discursively formed will consists in the fact that the reciprocal behavioral expectations raised to normative status afford validity to a *common interest* ascertained *without deception*. The interest is common because the constraint-free consensus permits only what *all* can want; it is free of deception because even the interpretations of needs in which *each individual* must be able to recognize what he wants become the object of discursive will-formation.

Habermas continues, "It is not the fact of ... pluralism that is here disputed but the assertion that it is impossible to separate by argumentation generalizable interests from those that are and remain particular." And further on, he claims that the moral principle of universalization "obliges each participant in a practical discourse to transfer his subjective desires into generalizable desires."[39]

These passages seem to reflect an ambiguity in the aims of practical discourse. On the one hand, practical discourse serves as a means simply of separating generalizable interests from particular interests. According to this account U serves as a bridge principle "which makes agreement in practical discourse always possible *if* matters can be regulated in the equal interests of all affected."[40] Here there is no assumption that matters always can be regulated in the interests of all affected. The claim seems to be simply that if a generalization of interests is achieved, we can justify the norms relevant to them. On the other hand, however, practical discourse is the means of transforming particular interests, need interpretations and desires *into* generalizable ones. Here the assumption seems to be that where matters cannot be regulated in the equal interests of all affected we have to allow all affected, not simply to test the generalizability of one another's interests, but one another's interpretations of them as well.

If one emphasizes the first account of the province of "U" and thus emphasizes the distinction between "normative statements" about the hypothetical "justice of actions and of norms" and "evaluative statements about subjective preferences" then one tries to acknowledge a form of pluralism. As Rawls and liberalism in general attempt to do, we allow for differences in subjective values and conceptions of the good while holding all to normative principles to which everyone can agree.[41] But we have had to question Habermas's strict divide between normative and evaluative questions since it appears that normative disputes can themselves engage differences in subjective preferences, evaluations and interpretations. Habermas's remarks on transforming subjective desires into universalizable ones might thus be understood as an attempt to retain the possibility of practical consensus in these instances by forging an identity in evaluations and interpretations. He includes under evaluative expressions one's interpretations of one's desires, feelings and needs, and now precisely these are to be universalized. The idea seems to be that if practical discourse cannot always be cleared of interpretive and evaluative issues and if rational moral consensus is nonetheless to remain a plausible idea, then particular interpretive and evaluative stances must themselves be subjected to the criterion of universalizability.

Habermas supplies a justification for this position. Following George Herbert Mead, he argues that as the subjects of moral theory we are socialized individuals. We form ourselves as individuals by learning to identify our particular needs and desires; but the terms in which we learn to interpret these are those of the speech community to which we belong. Certainly we can interpret our needs in ways that differ from the way others in the speech community understand theirs and we can also develop value standards at odds with those of the community. Nonetheless, the parameters for our differences and innovations are set by the language we speak and the cultural context in which we mature. These set the terms not only of what we accept but what we reject and how or why we reject it. Hence the community already participates in the formation of our identity and self-understanding. In allowing our need interpretations and desires to be the subject of practical discourse in which all participate we are therefore only acknowledging their linguistic, social and historical dimensions. "Needs and desires are interpreted in the light of cultural values and since these are always components of an intersubjectively shared tradition, the revision of need and desire interpreting values cannot be a matter over which the individual monologically disposes."[42]

It is not obvious, however, that although the description under which each perceives his interests must remain accessible to critique by others, this description must also be submitted to an, in principle, universal process of discursive will-formation. Why should I have to allow all those affected by a proposed norm to participate in the process in which I learn to understand my needs, desires and interests differently? And why is the revision here a matter for rational argument as opposed to therapeutic or aesthetic forms of discussion as Habermas originally describes them? Whereas it is plausible to claim that all those affected by a norm should be able to assent to it, it seems implausible to suggest that all those affected by a norm should also be able to assent to each other's need and interest interpretations. We are responsible for our interpretations and evaluations and responsible for the way in which our need interpretations, desires and qualitative assessments affect others. Hence, it makes sense to claim that we must be willing to test and revise them. But, with the notions of aesthetic criticism and therapeutic critique, Habermas himself seems to recognize that we cannot be simply argued out of them on the basis of their non-generalizability. They may be part of our cultural heritage and identity and, hence, although reasons may play a role in the process of revising them, they play only an indirect role. Neither the process of coming to interpret ourselves and our relations to others differently, nor the process of changing the evaluative terms with which we understand our world depends on the force of the better argument alone; rather both also involve transformations orientation that depend on experience and an education of our sensibilities.

Hermeneutics and Habermas

In recent essays such as "Modernity versus Postmodernity" and "Questions and Counterquestions," Habermas suggests a wider role for aesthetic critique than the one he gives it in *The Theory of Communicative Action*. Denying that it can be identified with "just one of the three validity claims" of truth, rightness or sincerity, he writes, "The one-to-one relationship which exists between the pre-scriptive validity of a norm and the normative validity claims raised in regulative speech acts is not a proper model for the rela-tion between the potential for truth of works of art and the trans-formed relations between self and world stimulated by aesthetic experience."[43] Rather, an aesthetic experience can be incorporated into an individual's or collective's life in such a way that it "reaches into and transforms the totality in which these moments are related to each other."[44]

It is not clear, however, that Habermas draws all the conse-quences of this circumstance for the idea of practical discourse. He concedes the impact an aesthetic experience can have, not just on our value standards, but on "our cognitive interpretations and nor-mative expectations." But if the domain of practical discourse can-not always be exempted from the consequences of interpretive and evaluative differences and if an aesthetic experience can change our understanding of the world and our moral obligations then we can give up on the idea of requiring universalizability from our inter-pretations of needs and desires. Instead, Habermas's expanded con-ception of aesthetic criticism seems to hint at the idea that although our interpretations and evaluative assessments legiti-mately resist the test of universal assent, this circumstance need not mean that they are immune to all forms of criticism or revi-sion. We do not need to assimilate evaluative and interpretive questions to practical ones because we can explore a more aesthe-tic process of change.

The standard hermeneutic claim of a theorist such as Rorty is that if we need to justify either our norms or our values and con-ceptions of the good, we need to do so only to those with whom we are substantively involved, those with whom we already share some part of our evaluative language and conceptions of the good. A corollary of this claim would seem to be that the possibility of revising our norms or values also depends on substantive relations we already have with others. If we are to examine or change our interpretations and evaluations, then the particular people asking us to examine them must matter to us; we must be able to trust and respect their interpretations and assessments and we must be will-ing to learn from them. Hence we are not, even ideally, free and equal participants in a practical discourse among all those affected. In the process of defining or revising who we are and what we take our needs, desires and goods to be we are rather individuals trying to refine our sensibilities and judgments and to educate and be educated by our friends and associates.

From this standard hermeneutic perspective this process has less to do with a discursive testing of general norms than with a mutual self- and value-definition. The force of the better argument takes second place to a shared development in our perceptions and understandings and second place, as well, to the judgment and sensitivity of those involved. Indeed, the very force of the various arguments and counter-arguments that arise in practical discourse depend upon an ongoing form of life that the participants already share. If the claims made by others are to matter to us at all, hermeneutics suggests, they cannot come from those about whom we do not care. A totalitarian critique of democracy is not one we can take seriously as members of a democratic society because we cannot have for a totalitarian regime the trust and respect that would allow us to care about its views of us. Similarly, if we are to challenge the morality of the Indian caste societies that Walzer discusses we must first establish some relationship with their members since only if we do so can they be expected to care about our criticisms and only if we do so can we expect them to try to change their sensibility, self-understanding and practice.

The contingency involved in these standard hermeneutic conclusions is dismaying however. Where we must depend on relations of trust, respect and commitment as well as on the processes of mutual and reciprocal self-definition these relations allow, we seem to be at the mercy of the speech community to which we belong and the friends we happen to have. We shall try to change our evaluations and interpretations to satisfy only those we already know and trust. But, if we are mistaken in these people, our self-definitional discussions with them will potentially degrade rather than educate us, as I have already remarked. Even if they do not, to the extent that we restrict those whose views we take seriously to those with whom we already share some sensibility and some part of an ongoing form of life, then we risk missing opportunities for self-scrutiny and change that can perhaps come from others. We may have substantive relationships that require us to take seriously the claims of those with whom we have these relationships. Moreover, the ongoing way of life we share with others may be the source as well as the focus of our interpretations and evaluations. Nevertheless, it is not clear that these circumstances can justify a hermeneutic limitation of those we should take seriously to those with whom we are already familiar.

For the most part, Habermas looks to the conditions of ideal speech for both normative justification and normative change. But his claims about aesthetic experience seem to indicate a different process of normative change, one that is neither as self-limiting as

Rorty's conception is, nor as frightening as the idea of subjecting our private need and interest interpretations to a universal, public, practical discourse is. In the next chapter, I shall explore the possibility of this kind of change, a change that incorporates both our normative expectations and our evaluative assessments. As usual I shall try to formulate my ideas by examining the work of others, in this case Charles Taylor, Alasdair MacIntyre and Hans-Georg Gadamer.

6

DEALING WITH INTERPRETIVE CONFLICT

In ending our discussion of Rawls's theory of justice, I suggested that his analysis of public reason might provide the starting point for a notion of hermeneutic conversation. Where political practices and institutions are thought to have their grounds in a common sense or public reason, critical reflection and revision become possible on the basis simply of "greater historical experience." The general question I want to explore in this chapter is whether the interpretive turn in debates over justice might be developed so as to have similar consequences. A conception of justice is now said not to issue from the truth of human nature or the requirements of human reason but, instead, simply from an understanding of the meaning of the society's own political traditions. If greater historical experience can transform what counts for that society as common sense it might also transform its understanding of the meaning of its political traditions and hence allow it to reflect upon the practices and conceptions of justice drawn from them. Moreover, if, as Rawls claims, the rival conceptions of justice drawn from an understanding of these political traditions can be "gradually modified and deepened by the contest between them,"[1] so too might rival interpretations of the political traditions, social goods and our historical actions and practices themselves. To explore this suggestion further we can contrast the views of Charles Taylor and Alasdair MacIntyre on conflict in social and political interpretation.

Taylor and the Idea of Accommodation

In an essay entitled "The Nature and Scope of Distributive Justice," Taylor begins where our reflections on Habermas's work left us off.[2] He argues that disputes over principles of distributive justice are always related to different interpretations and evaluations individuals have of the good for human beings and to different ideas of how society is to realize that good. In particular, he distinguishes a Lockean and atomistic view of this relation from an Aristotelian and social one. According to the first conception, the human good involves such specific goods as protection against attack from others and is thought to be only contingently related to human social association; in other words, the purpose of such association is to assist individuals in realizing their goods but the goods do not themselves require the association. In contrast, on the Aristotelian view, the human good is bound up with membership in a community and what the individual "acquires from this membership is not some aid in realizing his good but the very possibility of being an agent seeking that good."[3]

The principles of justice that follow from the Lockean view of the human good and social association turn on the notion of an equal fulfillment of the aims of society. For Locke, this equal fulfillment means an equal protection of the life, liberty and estates of individuals regardless of how inegalitarian the original distribution of property that is to be protected might be. Contemporary Lockeans use the idea of equal fulfillment to support what Taylor calls the contribution principle. The purpose of social association is no longer as much to protect property itself, as to enhance the individual productive capacities of the members of the association by combining and coordinating them with the capacities of others. Talents and abilities are of different values, however. "Thus on the principles of equal fulfilment of the aims of association, those of us with especially useful capacities, and who really use them to the full in our collaboration with others, ought to receive a greater share of the resultant product."[4] Justice rules out both a greater equality in income and a distribution of goods according to need. Talented people ought to be paid more than the untalented because of their greater contribution to the society and, hence, because of the way they enhance the inferior productive capacities of others; for the same reason, professionals ought to earn significantly more than those who perform jobs requiring less training and skill.

Opposed to the contribution principle is the idea stemming from an Aristotelian view of social association and human good according to which individuals within a society are equally indebted to one another for the form of life they share; all are equally respons- ible for sustaining that form of life and, for this reason, a larger de- gree of equality in the distribution of goods is required than is called for by the Lockean perspective. Whereas, in recent years, the Lockean view has been most systematically defended by Robert Nozick's *Anarchy, State and Utopia*,[5] Taylor identifies the Aristo- telian perspective with the views of both Rawls and Walzer.

Taylor claims that the conflict between Lockean and Aristotelian views is a dangerous one. As long as a society's economy is grow- ing, it may be possible to meet the distributive demands that issue from each. The society can use public funds to redress the most glaring inequities between groups while still assuring a high stan- dard of living for the talented and professional classes. When conti- nued growth becomes more difficult, however, grievances may increase that each side justifies through an implicit or explicit appeal to its particular interpretation of the good of social associ- ation. As Taylor explains:

> From both sides, the "system" comes to seem irrational and unjust. When the unskilled see how the doctors are able to command a large raise on already (to them) astronomical incomes, they conclude that the operative principle of distribution is according to blackmail power. This feeling is intensified when they discover the tax concessions that the middle class and the self-employed can often take advantage of. But from the other perspective, these raises and these concessions are seen as an all-too-grudging recognition of superior contribution, enter- prise and effort. On the contrary, from the standpoint of these privi- leged, their just differential is constantly being eroded by excessive taxation, because politicians succumb to the power of the mass vote.[6]

But Taylor argues that, despite the conflict between the two in- terpretations, each also corresponds to a "dimension of our social experience."[7] On the one hand we can legitimately claim, as Rawls does in justifying his second principle of justice, that the individ- ual's particular talents and capacities are a social asset and, hence, that only those inequalities are justified which also accrue to the ad- vantage of the least advantaged.[8] Nevertheless, in relying exclus- ively on this "balance of mutual indebtedness,"[9] we ignore that aspect of our understanding of the good of social association ac- cording to which it is to reward us as individuals, in proportion to our talents, hard work and enterprise. On the other hand, then, an individualistic interpretation of talents and capacities is also pos- sible. But to rely exclusively on *it* is to ignore other aspects of our understanding of the good of social association as well as important institutions and practices in line with this understanding. The individualistic perspective simply takes as a given the individual's understanding of himself or herself as an individual, as legitimately possessing his or her own aspirations and legitimately choosing freely his or her own life. It thereby forgets that this understanding of oneself as an individual depends upon a nexus of other social meanings: upon specific democratic institutions, upon certain shared ideas of citizenship, upon the possibility of a free exchange of ideas and upon a sense of responsibility for directing public affairs. Without these shared meanings, the sense of being an individual would be quite different, Taylor insists: "a sense of one's private tastes, a world of relationships cut off from the public world, a great desire to be left alone by the powers, whoever they are."[10] It follows that we can ignore the Aristotelian emphasis on our mutual indebtedness to one another for our shared social meanings and form of life only at some risk to the Lockean perspective on liberty itself.

Both Aristotelian and Lockean views, then, correspond to dimensions of our social experience and our understanding of the good of social association and each, nonetheless, leads to a different account of the principles of justice appropriate for us. How are we to adjudicate between these? The problem that arose in our discussion of Walzer's work with regard to differences in possible interpretations of specific social goods, in our discussion of Rawls's work with regard to differences in equally pragmatic interpretations of our strictly political traditions and in our discussion of Dworkin's work with regard to differences in our interpretation of the law arises here with regard to differences in the ways we understand the good of social association as a whole. If a hermeneutic political philosophy is concerned with understanding meaning — that of specific social goods, of political traditions, of the law or of the good of social association in general — how can we come to agree on what that meaning is? Taylor looks not for agreement at all but for some sort of accommodation:

> [S]ome things can be said in general about Western societies. All or most are or aspire to be republican societies sustaining the sense of individual liberty and common deliberation; and at the same time all or most are also experienced by their members as collaborative enterprises for the furtherance of individual prosperity. The first aspect is the basis for a principle of equal sharing, the second for ... the contribution principle. Justice involves giving appropriate weight to both these principles.[11]

Just how we are to give appropriate weight to both principles is not entirely clear, however. Taylor claims that the contribution principle must "be combined with more egalitarian considerations," but how? It would seem that we must move one way or the other. Either we must sustain the sense of commonality or solidarity by equalizing incomes or "sharing" or we must emphasize the rewards of hard work and individual enterprise by respecting differences in contribution. How can we do both?

It is possible to understand both Walzer and Rawls as trying to do just this by connecting the two different kinds of consideration to different aspects of the principles of justice. Walzer tries to accommodate, but limit, the validity of the contribution principle by tying it to the sphere of the market. Large differences in the wealth and income of members of a democracy are admissible as long as they pose no problems for the equal membership of all in the society and as long, therefore, as they cannot be used to purchase such goods as decent medical care, a decent education or political power. Rawls claims explicitly that his conception of justice is meant to reconcile Rousseauian and Lockean versions of the meaning of our traditions. His first principle of justice stresses the priority of the basic liberties as a means of satisfying the Lockean interpretation while the second principle of justice affords some attention to social solidarity in the idea that the most advantaged in the society should benefit only if their doing so also benefits the least advantaged.

Still, if these solutions succeed in satisfying the two conceptions of the good of social association that Taylor describes, they cannot succeed in accommodating differences in the way we interpret a single good or single action or practice. Even if we can allow for a free or relatively free market of commodities, for instance, without undermining the goods of social membership and solidarity, the question remains as to what we understand as a commodity. For those for whom the meaning of medical care is that of a need, distributions of it according to market imperatives will remain unjust. By the same token, for those for whom the American intervention in Vietnam constituted a form of imperialism, any similar intervention in Central America, for example, will remain a betrayal of America's "hopes and interests and self-image."[12] In general, it cannot satisfy those who interpret certain actions, goods or practices in a certain way to argue that the aspect of the meaning of our traditions with which they are concerned is embodied in some other actions, goods or practices. Politics is not always a question of balancing two interpretations by according each of them some dominion over some portion of the society's goods and practices, for we also often differ on how to understand just those goods and practices. MacIntyre suggests, more forcefully, that balancing and accommodating ought never to work, that it remains crucial to the health of any tradition that its members work through their interpretive differences rather than simply tolerating them.

Rational Justification and Interpretive Synthesis

In MacIntyre's view there is nothing either surprising or disasterous in the circumstance that members of a tradition can interpret the important beliefs, convictions and norms of that tradition in different ways. Nor is it either surprising or fatal that they possess different understandings even of which beliefs, convictions and norms are important. Rather MacIntyre defines what he calls a tradition of rational enquiry as "an argument extended through time in which certain fundamental agreements are defined and redefined."[13]

MacIntyre's focus here is thick traditions involving the social practices and moral life of a community. Only at the first stages of such traditions, he insists, are its fundamental agreements accepted in an unquestioned way. Traditions begin in historically contingent circumstances, with "the beliefs, institutions and practices of some particular community"[14] but they are then extended, developed and transformed through arguments and conflicts over what they mean, and how they can be best defended and extended. Traditions advance because their members actively and systematically take them up, because they try both to justify the beliefs and practices of the tradition and to resolve the problems that emerge in the course of these attempts. As MacIntyre puts this point, "A tradition of enquiry is more than a coherent movement of thought. It is such a movement in the course of which those engaging in that movement become aware of it and of its direction and in self-aware fashion attempt to engage in its debates and to carry its enquiries forward."[15]

Carrying a tradition forward, then, does not involve measuring its norms, practices and beliefs against an ideal standard, whether that of rational choice in the original position or that of rational consensus under the ideal speech situation. Rather, it involves two kinds of conflict or debate: "interpretive" debate within a tradition over "the meaning and rationale" of its fundamental agreements, and debate with "external" critics of the tradition who reject all or important aspects of these fundamental agreements.[16] Along the first dimension justifying norms, practices and ideas involves giving a narrative history of the tradition that can show the merit of a proposed resolution to perplexities or problems that have emerged with regard to those practices, norms and ideas. Along the second dimension, rational justification involves showing how aspects of the tradition are confirmed or need to be transformed because of the tradition's encounter with rival traditions.

Notwithstanding reservations MacIntyre has himself about Hegel's philosophy of history, his conception of the internal or vertical dimension of justifying norms and beliefs within a tradition is basically Hegelian. Systematic questions can begin to be raised within a tradition because its authoritative texts start to be interpreted in different ways, because internal inconsistencies between beliefs and practices become clear or because new situations arise that require reevaluations of old beliefs. The process of justifying solutions and revisions to these questions is a dialectical one in which one indicates how a given resolution preserves those aspects of a belief or practice that have withstood the questioning and transforms those that have not. To claim that a given belief is true or that a given practice is right is thus to claim that it is a solution that has thus far met the challenges to it and hence that, in light of the history of the issues involved, it is the best resolution to be as yet proposed.

To this extent justifying a norm, practice or belief involves placing it within a historical dynamic to which it belongs and showing how it offers a sustainable solution to certain perplexities or problems that arise in the course of that dynamic. Conversely, to call a belief false, or a practice or norm of action wrong, is to do so retrospectively; it is to locate a discrepancy between an older set of beliefs, norms or practices and a set of new evaluations and ideas. In Hegelian language, what was once the "in itself" of the object is now revealed as simply what was the "in itself for us" or the object as we once understood it. In taking up this "in itself" now, however, we can understand the ways in which it is inadequate and we take a new "in itself" as our object, one that is more adequate in just the respects in which our previous understanding failed. As MacIntyre writes:

> Those who have reached a certain stage in that development are then able to look back and to identify their own previous intellectual inadequacy or the intellectual inadequacy of their predecessors by comparing what they now judge the world, or at least part of it, to be with what it was then judged to be. To claim truth for one's present mindset and the judgments which are its expression is to claim that this kind of inadequacy, this kind of discrepancy, will never appear in any possible future situation, no matter how searching the enquiry, no

matter how much evidence is provided, no matter what developments in rational enquiry may occur. The test for truth in the present, therefore, is always to summon up as many questions and as many objections of the greatest strength possible; what can be justifiably claimed as true is what has sufficiently withstood such dialectical questioning and framing of objections.

The criterion of what has sufficiently withstood dialectical questioning is itself a standard produced through dialectical questioning and answering. As MacIntyre continues, "And those answers will compete rationally, just insofar as they are tested dialectically, in order to discover which is the best answer to be proposed so far."[17]

To this extent, it is crucial for MacIntyre, as it is for Hegel, that tradition-constituted enquiry remain "realistic" in that it view itself as progressing or moving through its debates over its fundamental agreements to an understanding of "the best answer to be proposed so far." In fact, MacIntyre thinks that a tradition must stagnate wherever it either accepts a more pluralistic conception of its differences or opts for a simply instrumentalist conception. The medieval attempt to justify one view of the heavens for theology and another for astronomy serves as one such example. Walzer's attempt to define justice differently for different spheres of social life might serve MacIntyre as another. In such cases, a tradition has reached the stage of internally debating different proposed solutions to its conflicts. Instead of attempting to work through them and achieve a best answer to the issues in question, however, it cuts off its own advance in favor of a simple appreciation of diversity. Alternatively, MacIntyre thinks that a tradition operating under the duress of different answers to its perplexities can enter into an "epistemological crisis."[18] In this case, members of the tradition retain a commitment to finding their way through and out of its conflicts to a best answer but cannot, at least for the moment, determine what this way is. Still, the test of the rationality of the tradition remains the extent of its commitment to weathering and transcending such crises by allowing for substantive debate and conflict, thereby allowing for the possibility of a best answer thus far.

For Hegel, of course, this process is a monolothic one so that the "in itself for itself" that emerges at the end of the process of a universal history represents the best answer for all time and all places. But this is the point at which MacIntyre parts company with Hegel, for he equates the idea of a best answer to be proposed thus far with neither universal history nor its end. In the first place, Mac-

Intyre argues, if we ever were to reach a state of "absolute knowledge," we would be unable to recognize it. Our task would remain that of dialectically testing our ideas and we could never know in advance that they were capable of withstanding all challenges, even if they were. In the second place, MacIntyre insists that traditions remain local affairs. Not only do they start in contingent circumstances, with the "particularities of language and social and natural environment" of a distinct community; they move in contingent and particular directions as well. The specificity of the issues that arise within a given tradition, the specificity of the trajectory its internal conflicts promote and the specificity of the ways in which it has historically attempted to resolve these conflicts precludes any idea of a teleologically conceived world history to which all traditions necessarily belong. "Traditions," MacIntyre writes, "fail the Hegelian test of showing that their goal is some final rational state which they share with all other movements of thought." They are, instead, "inhabited by Greeks or by citizens of Roman Africa or medieval Persia or by eighteenth-century Scots, who stubbornly refuse to be or become vehicles of the self-realization of *Geist*."[19]

If traditions remain stubbornly particular, however, it is not immediately clear that the external or horizontal dimension of justification between traditions to which MacIntyre points is possible. Justifying the norms, beliefs and practices of a tradition along this dimension is meant to involve showing how they stand up against challenges that arise in the encounter with another tradition and how the rejection of key agreements by external critics either requires revising those agreements or finding a way of defending their rationality against their critics. But if traditions are distinguished by the particularities of their language, public culture and "social and natural environment," it would seem that their concerns will be simply too particular to be accessible to any external review. Presumably the external critics of a tradition belong to their own traditions and presumably these traditions focus on issues that arise in the course of their particular historical development. Will the two traditions not therefore employ such different vocabularies and different criteria of truth and rationality that no productive dialogue between them is possible?

MacIntyre insists, in fact, that the more closely a community's language is tied to its beliefs, institutions and practices the more its use entails a range of substantive commitments and allegiances on the part of the speakers who employ it and the more its use therefore excludes the commitments and allegiances of the languages of other cultures and traditions. MacIntyre calls such a substantive language a language-in-use. The English name "Londonderry" and the Irish name "Doire Columcille" refer to the same location on a map. Nonetheless, because of their political and religious implications the location that one names is not the same as the location the other names. As MacIntyre explains, " 'Doire Columcille' embodies the intention of a particular and historically continuous Irish and Catholic community to name a place which has had a continuous identity ever since it became St Columba's oak grave in 564." In contrast, " 'Londonderry' embodies the intention of a particular and continuous English-speaking and Protestant community to name a settlement made in the seventeenth century." Hence, he insists, "To use either name is to deny the legitimacy of the other ... 'Londonderry' does not translate 'Doire Columcille' nor does 'St. Columba's oak grave', for in English there is no such name."[20]

But the mutual exclusion involved in this example also seems to preclude the external or horizontal strategy for rationally justifying a tradition's norms and beliefs. If using the name "Doire Columcille" simply precludes using the name "Londonderry" because of the history and nexus of allegiances connected with both, there seems to be no way that the use of one name could provide a way of testing the legitimacy or questioning the use of the other within the tradition to which it belongs; it seems, instead, irrelevant. But if two traditions are, on this account, simply inaccessible and irrelevant to one another, the same seems to hold along the dimension of what I have called vertical translation and justification as well. The internal justification of a belief or norm is meant to show that it is the best solution a tradition has yet found for its own difficulties and differences. But, as long as the language of a tradition reflects a language-in-use, a language entwined with a core set of beliefs, allegiances and commitments, it is not clear that we always share the difficulties and differences of even a previous stage of our own tradition. But, if we do not share its difficulties and conflicts, it is not clear how we can resolve them. The difficulty of translating, say, the fourteenth-century English of Lancashire into another period's or region's English-in-use and, hence, the difficulty of understanding its concerns will be the same as that of translating between a particular Irish-in-use and a particular English-in-use. In neither case will it be possible simply to match vocabularies and assume we hold issues in common. Rather, the vocabularies may involve radically divergent "semantic fields" and describe radically divergent issues and concepts, issues and concepts the meaning of which is simply obscured by the apparent identities in words. How is it possible, then, either to translate a language-in-use or to understand the challenge it presents to one's own tradition or language-in-use? How, in other words, is either the internal or the external form of justifying the norms and beliefs of a tradition possible?

MacIntyre's apparent answer to this question involves the idea of learning another language-in-use as a "second first language." The notion that one has learned another language when one can match the terms of that language with one's own corresponds only to the very first stages of learning another language. Understanding it more fully involves being able to think and act in it and, according to MacIntyre, this requires an immersion and resocialization within the ambit of its affiliations and common meanings. One needs to know not simply what word in one's own language corresponds to, say, "white" in the other, but what "white" means for the speakers of the other language and therefore what semantic space it occupies for them. As MacIntyre continues,

> Someone who knows that it is appropriate to assent to "Snow is white" if and when snow is white does not thereby evidence a grasp of "white" in English. Such a grasp would be evidenced by being able to say, for example, "Snow is white and so are the members of the Ku Klux Klan, and white with fear is what they were in snow-covered Arkansas last Friday."[21]

But, in order to able to use the word "white" in this way, one needs to know more than a list of English sentences and more than the translation of the color "white" in one's own language. One needs to be at home in the cultural history, experience and social practices of the culture that make its language a language-in-use. One needs to know how to go on and go further in the use of its expressions and this requires understanding their conceptual nuances, internal associations and implications. Only this thorough familiarity allows one to see what expressions one needs to formulate in one's first first language to capture the meaning expressed in one's second first language and vice versa; furthermore, only this kind of familiarity allows one to see which expression of one language cannot yet be expressed in the other.

How does this idea of a second first language resolve the problem we raised that, given their different concerns, semantic fields, allegiances and assumptions, one langauge-in-use must be simply irrelevant to the project of justifying the norms and beliefs of another? MacIntyre implies that the possibility of rational justification requires a certain interplay between traditions and languages-in-use that can, at the same time, remain distinct traditions and languages-in-use. If I am to justify my beliefs or norms of actions, there must be other beliefs and norms against which I can test them. On the one hand, therefore, I must know what these other beliefs and norms of action are; hence I must be able to translate them into my own language. On the other had I must be able to do so without losing their cultural specificity or their character of otherness. This means that I must know them in terms of the cultural and linguistic contexts that make them the beliefs and norms they are; and therefore, if I am to test my beliefs against them I must know them as a second first language.

It is not the fact of possessing its own concerns and issues that makes a culture or tradition ethnocentric, MacIntyre suggests; it is rather assuming the adequacy of a word-by-word translation of another language into one's own first language, failing to recognize differences in use and thereby missing the opportunity of testing the validity of one's own norms and beliefs against those of the other language. To assume that one's own language-in-use is adequate to capturing all that can be expressed in any other language-in-use is an illusion that MacIntyre claims modern universalism shares with Hegel. It assumes all languages are part of a larger dynamic and hence intertranslatable. Such an illusion simply gives up on the possibility of understanding the possible challenges that another tradition and language-in-use can bring to one's own way of thinking.

Thus, as long as a language is tied to a background of shared communal beliefs, the justification of its beliefs, standards of rationality and norms of action must take the form of a confrontation between two languages-in-use, where the possibility of the confrontation depends, first, on acknowledging the possibility of real differences and real incommensurabilities between the two languages and, second, on a thorough and internal familiarity with each. A language-in-use must be incompatible with one's own in order to provide a foil against which to test one's own. But one must also be able to understand the way it actually does illuminate the merits and demerits of one's own and, for MacIntyre, this means that one must understand it as a second first language.

It is worth emphasizing that a second first language can serve this justificatory function, for MacIntyre, only if it is recognized as a language-in-use. Where a language has become "universalized" or, in other words, where it no longer entails a background of tradition-bound, substantive commitments of its own, it may be able more easily to accommodate other languages than a language-in-use can. Nevertheless, it does so at the cost of understanding the way in which different languages-in-use are languages-in-use and hence at the cost of being able to understand the distinctiveness of the claims and perspectives they embody. To the extent that languages lose the distinctiveness of their world views and frames of reference they are unable either to challenge or to define an independent foil for one another through which they can test and try to justify their beliefs. To deny the differences necessary to either external or internal debate by assuming the a priori possibility of leveling all linguistic frameworks within a universal commensurability is thus, on this view, just to give up on rational justification.[22] Indeed, MacIntyre contends that "the only rational way for adherents of any tradition to approach intellectually, culturally, and linguistically alien rivals is one that allows for the possibility that in one or more areas the other may be rationally superior to it in respect precisely of that in the alien tradition which it cannot as yet comprehend."[23]

This aspect of MacIntyre's account of the rationality of traditions recalls our earlier remarks on the capacity to learn from what we are trying to understand, for MacIntyre seems to consider precisely this potential for self-education to be the crucial aspect of dialogue within or between traditions. In trying to justify our social, political and legal norms, we must presuppose that we can learn from alien traditions and alien perspectives with regard to the issues with which we are concerned. We must suppose that their norms and their perspective can illuminate the issues in a way that is significant for us and, indeed, that this illumination can come from just what we do not initially understand about that perspective. The burden of interpretation falls to the interpreter, to the person concerned with the legitimacy of his or her own beliefs and norms. The task is to find in a second first language a worthy opponent to our own tradition. We do so not by assuming that its members must really mean what we already mean, but rather by assuming the opposite. The attempt to justify our beliefs and traditions involves the constant attempt to understand alien meanings under the assumption that they might say something other than what we already know or believe and might be therefore important for us as a challenge that pushes us either to clarify our thoughts and develop our norms or to reject them and start again.

From the point of view, then, of its encounter both with alien traditions and with alien versions of itself, whether contemporary or historical, the rationality of a tradition consists in its willingness to be refuted. It must be willing to test itself against other traditions and other notions of itself and to accept new perspectives if it cannot successfully defend its old ones under the impact of its new circumstances and understanding. But these requirements mean that the continued rationality of a tradition also requires continued conflict with others and debate with itself. In each case it must acknowledge the possibility of viewpoints other than its own. Hence it must accept, it would seem, a kind of interpretive pluralism as the basis of its own strength and rationality. Indeed, it would seem that the kinds of interpretive debates within a tradition that we have considered in this book — that between Walzer and Dworkin over the meaning of medical care in the United States or that between Rawls and either a political "Aristotelian" or a libertarian over the meaning of democratic politics, or that between Walzer and Rawls on the one hand, and Nozick, on the other, over the aims of social association — are instances of just the kind of debates that could constitute, for MacIntyre, a tradition "in good working order."[24] Just as the rationality of a tradition requires that it test itself against other traditions and be willing to learn from them, the rationality of one strand of a tradition seems to involve its testing itself against and learning from other strands of the same tradition. Moreover, just as one tradition must assume that another might be rationally superior to it, one interpretive perspective within a tradition must assume that another can offer it insights into interpreting shared social meanings. Hence, just as alien traditions would seem therefore to need each other for purposes of self-testing and self-education, MacIntyre's account seems also to suggest that a single tradition needs a plurality of interpretations of itself.

In *Whose Justice? Which Rationality?*, having considered the Aristotelian, Augustinian and Scottish Enlightenment traditions in depth, MacIntyre does offer a sketch of the tradition of liberal individualism in which the debates I enumerated would seem to have their home. At the same time, however, he contrasts liberal individualism to the perspective of traditions and suggests that the interpretive pluralism of the former has nothing to do with either reason or rational justification.

The Tradition of Liberal Individualism

Liberalism begins, according to MacIntyre, as an attempt to found a social order in which individuals could be emancipated from the "contingency and particularity of tradition." That is, it tries to establish a political, legal and economic framework that allows individuals with different heritages and different conceptions of the good life to live together under the same set of rationally justifiable principles of justice. As MacIntyre explains, the presupposition of this order is that: "Every individual is to be equally free to propose and to live by whatever conception of the good he or she pleases, derived from whatever theory or tradition he or she may adhere to unless that conception of the good involves reshaping the life of the rest of the community in accordance with it."[25]

For MacIntyre this final qualification is devastating since it removes conceptions of the good from the realm of possible rational justification. Liberalism accepts the Enlightenment's standard of justification according to which a notion of the good could be justified only if it were a good all rational agents could accept. Since, however, it ultimately can find no good to fill this place, all goods are relegated to the domain of mere subjective preference. But this decision means that liberalism is just as much a tradition as those it opposes. It has its own conception of the good: namely, one in which conceptions of the good are purely private affairs. They are not admissible into the public discourse as rationally justifiable claims to the good for human beings in general; neither, therefore, are they admissible as proposals for reshaping the community as a whole. Liberalism also has its own conception of practical reason. Since no conception of the good is rationally justifiable and since all are, instead, simply preferences, it becomes irrational to pursue one at the expense of all others. As MacIntyre quotes Rawls: "Human good is heterogeneous because the aims of the self are heterogeneous. Although to subordinate all our aims to one end does not strictly speaking violate the principles of rational choice ... it still strikes us as irrational or more likely as mad."[26] Finally, liberalism has its own distinctive conception of justice. If conceptions of the good are not to be treated as truth claims, the role of a conception of justice is merely to find a way of neutralizing or resolving any conflicts between the preferences of different individuals that might occur.

MacIntyre distinguishes four levels in the liberal view of justice. There is first the level at which individuals and groups express their opinions and attitudes. Characteristic of these opinions and attitudes is not just that they themselves conflict with others, that some groups, for example favor a woman's right to choose an abortion and that some equate abortion with infanticide or that some groups support affirmative action policies while others oppose them. In a liberal individualist order, the set of assumptions to which the different groups appeal to support their views also differ. Hence, in the examples above, some groups appeal to notions of divine law, some to notions of inalienable human rights and still others to Aristotelian conceptions of human good.

MacIntyre insists that the "only *rational* way in which these disagreements could be resolved would be by means of philosophical enquiry aimed at deciding which out of the conflicting sets of premises, if any is true."[27] But within the liberal tradition not only can individual claims to what the good life is for human beings not be understood or appear as validity claims in the sphere of public discussion; the same restrictions apply to the set of assumptions that would be used to support these claims. They, too, are reduced to subjective preferences. And, since liberal individualism thus denies that any conception of the good or any set of assumptions can be true or false, where conflicts occur they must be resolved by other means. Thus, a second level of the liberal conception of justice involves "tallying and weighing ... expressions of preferences."[28] People vote, answer consumer choice surveys and respond to public and public opinion polls. This second level presumes the rationality of the procedures and rules for counting votes and scoring surveys but a third level in the liberal view of justice involves philosophical and quasi-philosophical debate over just such rules and over principles of justice in general.

Although no resolutions are forthcoming on this third level, MacIntyre suggests that it has two functions. First, it is "socially effective" in indicating that if the relevant set of principles for adjudicating between preferences has not yet been finally discovered or implemented, discovery and implementation remain central goals of the social order. Second, in thereby allowing for continued debate, this third level provides the justification for the fourth level in which conflicts of preference are resolved by the formal legal system. The role of this system is to provide decisions on such conflicts without invoking an overall theory of human good and it does so by appealing to any of the various positions in the third level debates over principles of justice. Indeed, MacIntyre concludes that the characteristic mark of liberalism is that it does not seek a real resolution of conflict in genuine philosophical inquiry. Rather, liberalism simply accepts the verdicts of the legal system, verdicts that have been formed through appeals to whatever position in the philosophical debates seems to support them most easily at the time. "The lawyers not the philosophers are the clergy of liberalism," MacIntyre claims.[29]

If liberalism is a tradition with its own conceptions of human good, practical reason and justice, for MacIntyre, its specific conceptions of these nevertheless ensure that it is a bankrupt tradition. A rational tradition progresses because its conflicts and interpretive debates have real objects; they are conflicts and debates not only over the meaning but over the rationale of fundamental agreements concerning the good, justice and reason. Where two positions on these agreements differ, the conflict between them is understood as a serious conflict, as a conflict for which a substantive resolution is urgent. MacIntyre's central example is Aquinas's synthesis of Augustinian and Aristotelian traditions within the framework of a unified metaphysical theology. In this case, it was crucial both that Aquinas had a thorough, if accidental familiarity with each tradition, that the Aristotelian tradition constituted a second first language for him, and that he had the ability to recognize that each tradition was inadequate as it stood. But he could only recognize these inadequacies, according to MacIntyre, because he presumed that the conflict between the two traditions was a genuine one and because he was therefore committed to a concept of a truth or best answer to the discrepancies between the two traditions that could transcend their respective inadequacies while preserving their truths. Conversely, had he either proposed an instrumentalist solution, arguing for the adequacy of each tradition for different purposes, or taken a perspectivist position, treating each as simply different world-views that no "fact of the matter" could adjudicate, his own tradition of Augustinian Catholicism could not have progressed. The advance of this tradition rather required that it recognize the Aristotelian tradition as a real challenge and that it therefore attempt to find some solution to the conflict that could be seen as superior, for clearly defined reasons, to the perspectives of either tradition on its own.

Liberalism, however, reduces all conceptions of the good, as well as all the philosophical premises on which these conceptions rest, to subjective preferences. Hence, the universalized language it adopts denies any real incompatibility between languages-in-use and, thus, any way that they can really challenge one another. Similarly, liberalism's conceptions of human good and practical rationality deny the reality of any important conflict between ideas of the good or ways of life. All are simply different conceptions and the role of political principles of justice is to find ways of balancing and accommodating all or most of them as long as they remain purely private views. For MacIntyre this perspective means that pluralism and toleration replace the impulse toward rational synthesis. For liberalism "less and less importance has been attached to arriving at substantive conclusions and more and more to continuing the debate for its own sake."[30] Liberalism is a tradition that makes debate interminable, domesticates epistemological crises and thereby itself becomes inert.

This conclusion suggests that the problems with which we have been concerned in this book, namely, those of dealing with interpretive conflicts and doing so in a rational way, might be more properly viewed as problems of political liberalism. On this view, it is because liberalism reduces ideas of the good to mere preferences that contemporary disputes over the justice of particular actions, practices and institutions can be neither resolved nor transcended. Under liberalism, neither conflicting conceptions of justice nor conflicting ideas of the good can be viewed as genuine challenges to each other and this means that the different sides can be only weighed and accommodated in some such manner as Taylor suggests. Without genuine challenges, however, the different conceptions of the good and ideas of justice must remain untested and, hence, irrational. The courts may be the ultimate arbiter of justice in a liberal order as Dworkin suggests. But, in MacIntyre's view, the possibility of rationally justifying that order has been subjectivistically precluded.

Just as Habermas's account of ideal speech does, MacIntyre's account of the contest between and within traditions bears some affinities with John Stuart Mill's defense of free discussion in *On Liberty*. Habermas is closer to Mill in his focus on justifying universal rights and principles, but the idea that we subject our opinions, even those over ethics and religion, to challenges from others is one MacIntyre holds up against a more contemporary and subjectivistically reduced liberalism. Of course, MacIntyre's concern is not the universal validity of a set of opinions, but its justification within the tradition to which it belongs and the justification of that tradition against others to, at least, the temporary satisfaction of its members. MacIntyre implies that when we test our views against those of others we are not necessarily attempting to convert them to our view. We are rather trying to determine whether we should be converted to theirs. This we cannot do by simply tolerating diversity, as contemporary liberalism does on MacIntyre's account. We make our determinations instead by engaging in real conflict and debate. MacIntyre's suggestion here as well as the suggestion about a hermeneutic education we made in chapter 5 owes much to Gadamer and, in particular, owes much to Gadamer's notion of anticipating completeness (*der Vorgriff der Vollkommenheit*) to which I now turn.

Gadamer's Anticipation of Completeness

As we have seen, a hermeneutic understanding of a text begins with the assumption that it is internally coherent. Indeed, hermeneutics suggests that the adequacy of any interpretation of meaning depends upon its capacity to show how a text composes a unified whole, or, in other words, how its parts are integrated with one another to form a self-consistent meaning. Such a hermeneutic approach does not deny that a given text might form no self-consistent whole; nonetheless, it suggests that inconsistencies can only appear as the specific inconsistencies they are understood to be under some general interpretation of the meaning of the whole from which they are supposed to deviate. Hermeneutic approaches to social interpretation make the same presumption. An interpreter might contend that the overall meaning of political democracy is such as to imply that property does not by itself confer political power on its owner. Where political power is conferred upon factory-owners, in that they control the working lives and freedom of their employees, this practice introduces a contradiction into the "text" of democracy. As in textual interpretation, the idea here is that we can use various parts of a history or social context to understand the meaning of the whole and that we can use the whole to understand the meaning and potential deviations of the parts. Each serves as a check on the other by requiring a full integration of part and whole.

Gadamer's notion of anticipating completeness goes a step further, moving, in this regard, in the same direction that Dworkin's criterion of best light could move if it were uncoupled from Dworkin's theoretical orientation and given a more immanent thrust. According to Gadamer, the point of any serious attempt to understand the meaning of a text or text analogue must be to achieve a better understanding of the issues and questions with which we are concerned. In other words, we must suppose that the texts or text analogues we are studying can be not only internally coherent but also illuminating, that they can educate us over some subject matter, answer a question we have or clarify some issue. Conversely, if a text or text analogue seems to have nothing to say to us, if we can learn nothing from it with regard to the concerns we share with it or if the distinctions it makes make no sense to us, it may be that we have simply understood the text or the distinctions poorly.

In this way, the "anticipation of completeness" adds another condition to the adequacy of interpretation. If one reason to suspect a given understanding of a text or text analogue is that it claims that the text has no unity, another is that it claims that the text can have no meaning or significance for us. Naturally, just as a text may ultimately prove to be incoherent, it might also prove to be either irrelevant to us or misleading with regard to our concerns. For example, we may be simply unable to make sense out of a principle of justice that rests on a temporal distinction between emotional injury suffered at the time of an accident and emotional injury suffered later but because of the accident. From a Gadamerian perspective, however, the rejection of such a principle is justified only if it is the result of a genuine attempt to grasp both the coherence of the position and the way it might enlighten us with regard to some issue. A genuine attempt to understand is one that is engaged in attempts similar to those MacIntyre describes: it tries to find insights in another's position and is open to the challenge these insights can bring to its own perspective.

This account of textual understanding further collapses the distinction between understanding and application we looked at in the last chapter. When we are trying to understand a text, we are trying to understand what it means for us, given who we are, the history we are part of, the assumptions we have thus far made and the issues in which we take an interest. This application to a particular situation is clearest in the law: as we have seen, we cannot understand the meaning of the equal protection clause without grasping what it means for specific cases such as segregated schooling. Similarly, we cannot understand a text without conceiving of it in personal terms, applying its perceptions and moral evaluations to our own, assessing them in terms of our own and, to that extent, entering into a dialogue or virtual dialogue with it. But if all understanding requires specific applications, then it is itself a specific understanding, a particular dialogue with particular concerns. As such, the meaning of a text for us, given our concerns and situation, cannot rule out the possibility of its possessing a different meaning for others, given their different concerns and situation. Interpretations of meaning are never exhaustive. A text will refer to different experiences and issues for different generations of interpreters and may have different meanings for different members of the same generation. Hence we can never claim eternal truth for our interpretations but must rather hold them open to changes in historical circumstances, in our concerns and in the issues that arise. Moreover, we must recognize that the strength of our own interpretations may depend upon our ability to learn from the alternative ones of others.

What relevance does this conclusion have for hermeneutic political theory? Such a theory takes its task to be that of interpreting shared social meanings, public values and common political traditions with the aim of formulating a conception of justice that is congruent with these. It no longer claims to be articulating universally valid principles of justice or principles grounded on a priori moral standards. This transformation means that significant differences in the principles that different hermeneuticists defend can no longer be understood as differences over universal principles of justice or over those principles that are uniquely well justified.

Rather, disputes over principles of justice reflect differences either over which institutional arrangements comply with a given society's public political culture or over what that public political culture itself means. But this transition from disputing claims to truth to recognizing our differences as interpretive differences is crucial, for once we understand our disputes in this way we can no longer contend that only one result can be right. A hermeneutic political theory allows us to conceive of our conceptions of justice as constrained interpretations of our democratic traditions, institutions and practice. But our interpretations will never be exclusive because there will always be other ways of understanding the experience, different experiences to connect it to and so on. Consequently, because there is nothing non-interpretive about our own interpretations, we can recognize that we might learn from others. Indeed, by attempting seriously to understand the insights such other perspectives provide, we can begin to educate ourselves and to revise or develop our understanding.

It is not clear, then, that we ought to condemn, as MacIntyre does, a pluralistic society that simply allows for different interpretive stances to its own shared meanings rather than trying to resolve them. To be sure, by interpretive stances we do not now mean subjective preferences, but we can give up on a synthetic best answer thus far to which we can all agree and allow for different interpretive emphases in our understanding of our political culture and historical traditions because each of these different interpretive stances can pose a challenge to the others as a perspective from which they might learn. Each perspective may develop along its own lines and no consensus may develop within a tradition any more than one need develop between them, as Hegel (and Mill) assume. Yet, in concert with the others, each perspective can refine itself and become both more differentiated and more aware of the internal difficulties with which it must deal.

The sort of challenge that arises here is akin to the form of aesthetic criticism that Habermas outlines. An interpretation of a work of art that differs from our own presents a challenge to us as an interpretation against which we must reexamine our own precisely because ours is "just" an interpretation as well. We do not, in the aesthetic sphere, insist upon the uniqueness of our interpretations. Rather because we can recognize both of two different interpretations as interpretations, we also try to see what in the work each alternative interpretation illuminates, how each illuminates it and what each particular illumination reveals about the work. Both interpretations may be "true" to the work in their own fashions. In taking seriously the interpretive insights of the other, however, we can begin to improve our own. The result might be deemed an enriched one in that, whether we adopt insights of the other perspective or not, we have learned through our encounter with it.

For political theory, this claim means that its task perhaps should not be to adjudicate between different interpretations of the meaning of our political heritage. Perhaps it should not be trying to forge a consensus or synthesis of interpretations. Perhaps it should be trying, rather, to discover what each interpretation can learn from the others and to encourage a kind of hermeneutic conversation in which different interpretations can become more educated, refined and sophisticated through their "contest" with the others. In a conversation of this kind each interpretive stance may retain its distinctiveness; it can also help to develop and enrich the others and, in turn, be developed and transformed by them. We need not agree with each other in the end, but we can all come to recognize the partial and one-sided character of our initial positions and incorporate into our more considered views the insights we have come to learn by trying to understand other interpretations of our history and experience. The important question, then, is no longer which interpretation of our history and experience is correct because none is exhaustively correct. The important question is, rather, how or why our interpretations differ and what new insights into the meaning of our traditions we might glean from the attempt to understand the cogency of interpretations different from our own.

This notion of a hermeneutic conversation may go beyond the point of Gadamer's own "anticipation of completeness" in that it seems to provide some substitute for Kantian foundations. If we are now to give up on justifying the norms and practices of our shared substantive life in terms of unconditioned principles external to it, we can allow for assessments and refinements of our interpretations within the hermeneutic domain itself, in terms of the challenges and spurs to development our differing interpretations provide for one another. This notion allows for challenges to our self-understanding that issue from beyond the sphere of those with whom we are already involved. The hermeneutic restriction we considered in the last chapter, that we can and need justify our self-understanding only to those who already share a large part of our sensibility, history and evaluative language, no longer holds. Instead, the idea of a hermeneutic conversation opens up the possibility of learning, not only from members of our own culture, but from groups with radically different histories and sensibilities. We can now approach these with the same "anticipation of completeness" with which we approach texts and the interpretations of those we know and trust. That is, we can approach them, as Mac-Intyre suggests, as at least potential repositories of insight into meaning.

Thus, the discussion of different interpretations of our goods and practices need not take the form either of practical discourse or of hermeneutic justification as understood by such theorists as Rorty and Williams. We need be neither Kantians nor communitarians in moral and political theory. Once we make the interpretive turn, the justification of our principles becomes dialogic and the scope of the dialogue becomes unlimited. We need neither try to purify our discourse of interpretive elements nor talk only to those who already share our interpretations. Instead we can try to learn from the understanding of meaning others possess and try to develop our own understanding through conversation with them. Such learning can be reciprocal. In our dialogue with one another over our interpretations and evaluations we need not seek consensus. The point from both sides is to make sure their own interpretations are as compelling and inclusive as they can be. Two interpreters may understand a work of art differently and they may draw different implications from their conversations with each other. Similarly, in politics we shall have to allow for an interpretive domain that, although enriched by conversation and deepened by the contest between interpretations, can remain pluralistic not only at the start of conversation but at the finish.

Of course, this conclusion may seem to leave a crucial question not only unanswered but unanswerable. The interpretive pluralism that we are now commending is not a pluralism with regard only to questions of the good life. It is a pluralism that also affects the questions of what principles or norms are appropriate for us and indeed of who we are and want to be. But if we are now to reap the benefits of this kind of interpretive pluralism rather than resolving it, what is a pluralistic society to do about the concrete issues on which it disagrees? How can the United States, for example, accommodate both those interpretations of medical care that understand it as a need and those interpretations that understand it as a commodity? What do we do about debates over abortion or Vietnam? Even if we recognize that a conversation between two contrasting interpretations may be important to the strength and cogency of both interpretations, a community must still move in some direction in its policies and practices and it is not clear that we will always be able to satisfy two opposed interpretations at once.

There is a more serious problem with our conclusions as they stand. If the idea of a hermeneutic conversation allows us to escape the claustrophobic confines of a Rortian hermeneutics it seems to encounter perhaps the very difficulty that Rorty is trying to avoid. For if we are no longer to try to learn only from those we already know and trust, because doing so limits our opportunities for self-education, it seems equally dangerous to assume that we should try to learn from just anyone. Will certain interpretive positions not serve to coarsen rather than refine us if we really attempt to take them seriously as potential possessors of insight into meaning? Are there not certain positions, such as a defense of slavery, that we can claim have already been sufficiently debated in our common history that we need no longer entertain? Are there not others that we cannot dismiss as easily or clearly but that are equally perverse? Can we prevent ourselves, before the fact, from learning from our conversations with racists or sexists or fascists? Put differently, is there some way we can monitor what we learn or from whom we learn it? These questions, of course, are similar to the questions we raised at the end of our consideration of Dworkin's work and that led us to consider Habermas's discourse ethics. We saw that this discourse ethics could not help us resolve interpretive differences that enter into practical discourse itself. Still, if we must now accept the idea of a hermeneutic conversation in which the goal is no longer only consensus, might not Habermas's work provide us with rational standards *for* this conversation?

7

HERMENEUTIC CONVERSATION AND THE CRITIQUE OF IDEOLOGY

If we look briefly at John Stuart Mill's discussion of free thought and discussion in *On Liberty* we can understand the distance the hermeneutic turn has taken us. Mill's concern is the truth of opinions, about which there are two possibilities. First, if our opinions are false, free discussion grants us the opportunity of exchanging them for true ones; second, if an opinion "is right" already, free discussion offers "almost as great a benefit, the clearer perception and livelier impression of truth produced by its collision with error."[1] Under the first of these two possibilities, if we simply assume that our opinions are true and our judgment infallible then we deny the possibility of progress. We can never allow our own beliefs to be corrected because we refuse to listen to or tolerate opinions other than our own. "There is the greatest difference," Mill asserts, "between presuming an opinion to be true because, with every opportunity for contesting it, it has not been refuted, and assuming its truth for the purpose of not permitting its refutation." Nor can false opinions be corrected through experience alone, for, Mill asserts, discussion is necessary to show us how that experience is to be interpreted. "Wrong opinions and practices gradually yield to fact and argument; but facts and arguments, to produce any effect on the mind, must be brought before it."[2]

Second, even where an opinion does not need to be corrected, unless it is "fully, frequently and fearlessly discussed," Mill argues, "it will be held as a dead dogma not a living truth." He concedes that discussion may be unnecessary with regard to such subjects as geometry and mathematics in general since, in these cases, "all the argument is on one side. There are no objections and no answers to objections." In cases where a difference of opinion is possible, however, "the truth depends on a balance to be struck between two sets of conflicting reasons." Such a balance is required in natural philosophy where "there is always some other explanation possible of the same facts." And it is even more necessary in "subjects infinitely more complicated" such as "morals, religions, politics, social relations and the business of life."[3] In these cases one has always to study opinions that conflict with one's own and show how one's own belief, if it is correct, withstands the challenges they mount, what fallacies these other beliefs involve and so on. Holding to one's correct beliefs in a rational manner involves not only understanding the reasons that support those beliefs but being able to refute the contrary reasoning of others. "He who knows only his own side of the case knows little of that. His reasons may be good and no one may have been able to refute them. But if he is equally unable to refute the reasons on the opposite side, if he does not so much as know what they are, he has no ground for preferring either opinion."[4]

Despite this analysis, Mill does not conclude that a diversity of contrasting opinions is necessary to the vitality of the truth of any. Rather, he asserts that "the well-being of mankind may almost be measured by the number and gravity of the truths which have reached the point of being uncontested." This "gradual narrowing of the bounds of diversity of opinion" is both "inevitable and indispensable." Still, this narrowing can lead to the stultification of true opinion, to its being held as "dead dogma" rather than "living truth". Hence, we need some substitute for a genuine contrast of positions, "some contrivance for making the difficulties of the question as present to the learner's consciousness as if they were pressed upon him by a dissentient champion, eager for his conversion." Mill points to Plato's dialogues and the school disputations of the Middle Ages as examples of successful contrivances, concluding that "if there are any persons who contest a received opinion, or will do so if law and opinion will let them, let us thank them for it, open our minds to listen to them, and rejoice that there is someone to do for us what we otherwise ought, if we have any regard to either the certainty or the vitality of our convictions, to do with much greater labor for ourselves."[5]

This defense of the importance of free discussion has obvious affinities with the account of hermeneutic conversation I gave in the last chapter as well as with the emphasis on dialogue we found in the work of both Habermas and MacIntyre, as I have already suggested. But Mill's defense is closest to Habermas's account of discourse in that it understands the subject of discourse or discussion to be the truth of an opinion or, presumably, the rightness of a norm. Moreover, just as Habermas explicitly ties the justification of principles or norms to a universal consensus, Mill anticipates such a consensus in the idea of a "gradual narrowing of the bounds of diversity of opinion." MacIntyre also looks to conversation as the medium of rational justification. Still he stresses that agreements as to truth and rightness are always bound to particular traditions. The way in which traditions test the rationality of their agreements is through a dialogue with other traditions in which comparison is made possible by the possession of a first and second first language. Such dialogue between traditions does not, however, mean that they become part of a universal history or a linear progress of truth. For MacIntyre, each tradition justifies itself to the satisfaction of its own current members and not according to universal principles of rationality.

For its part, a hermeneutic political philosophy might understand the task of justification in a way that can be conceived of as combining MacIntyre's analysis with Gadamer's "anticipation of completeness." The subject matter of a hermeneutic conversation, so conceived, is neither principles of justice to which everyone could agree nor the truth of opinions. It is rather the possibility of different interpretations of a tradition and of the practices, experiences and actions it includes. The goal of such conversation is not as much an agreement over norms as a plurality of enriched, more differentiated and more educated interpretations. Indeed, the necessity of conversation issues precisely from the interpretive character of various understandings of meaning. For Mill, discussion is necessary because our opinions of truth are fallible, because we can never be certain we are correct or that "the opinion we are endeavoring to stifle is ... false ..."[6] If, however, the subject of conversation is different interpretations of the meaning of a specific history, set of social goods, political tradition or the like, then the issue is not the fallibility of the opinions expressed but the inevitable partiality of the interpretations. That is, if we acknowledge the interpretive character of our conceptions of justice, then we must also recognize that they can never reflect an exhaustive account of the meaning of our history and that there will always be other equally legitimate interpretations emphasizing different aspects of it. Both diversity and dialogue, then, are necessary, not because we could be wrong, but because we can never be wholly correct or rather because the issue is no longer as much one of rightness or wrongness as one of continuing revision and reform.

In chapter 6, I asked why we could not extend this conception of hermeneutic conversation to the tradition of liberalism that Mac-Intyre finds so conceptually bankrupt. According to MacIntyre, the problem with liberalism is that it reduces conceptions of the good to subjective preferences and hence no longer conceives of them according to criteria of rationality. Criteria of rationality are supposed to be applicable to issues of justice but since principles of justice in a liberal regime are only principles for balancing irrational conceptions of the good, they, too, become irrational. MacIntyre argues that the courts do rely on principles of justice in deciding individual cases in law but they rely on random principles geared to specific issues and hence do not supply any greater rationality to the process of political decision-making in a liberal order. Hence, the liberal tradition may or may not adopt Rorty's hermetic advice and give up on any attempt to justify its principles of justice to outsiders; on MacIntyre's view, since it is arbitrary which principles predominate within it at a given time, it has already abandoned any real attempt to justify these principles to itself.

Still, if we focus on the interpretive character of both conceptions of the good and principles of justice it is not clear that a liberal regime need abandon every form of rational justification or, at least, self-education. Once we argue that justifiable conceptions of justice are those that are faithful to a community's political and historical traditions and to the meanings of its social goods, we must recognize that others might understand these traditions and social meanings differently than we do. At issue is not a purchase on truth but a reading of meaning where different interpreters in politics, as in literary studies, can legitimately emphasize different interpretive contexts, different interrelations between different meanings and so on. Consequently, we must also acknowledge the possibility that members of a democratic political culture will derive different conceptions of justice from their different understandings both of the important meanings of this culture and of which meanings are important. Indeed, we must acknowledge that outsiders will understand these meanings differently as well. But, once we recognize these possibilities, we can also acknowledge that we might learn from alternative interpretations and, indeed, that we can learn from them whether they belong to members of our own society or to external critics. By working through these alternative interpretations and assuming their possible insights into dimensions of meaning, we can reflect upon our own interpretations and revise or develop them more fully. Our own understanding can become more differentiated, sophisticated and nuanced by incorporating what it takes as the interpretive insights of others and protecting itself from what it still, after some consideration, takes as their lacunae.

Although the idea of a hermeneutic conversation among the various members of a liberal order might thus rescue this order from the kind of irrationalism MacIntyre fears, the idea seems to risk another form of irrationalism. Abandoning the ideal of a universal and rational consensus over norms of action and principles of justice means that we must confront a problem neither Mill nor Habermas must face. For how can hermeneutic conversation, as described above, guarantee that it *will* have a self-educational character? Mill simply assumes that the progress of free discussion is the progress of truth and rationality, whereas Habermas imposes certain conditions on the kind of dialogue that can guarantee a rational consensus. But, if we must be open to learning from different interpretations once we acknowledge the interpretive nature of our own conceptions of justice, it appears that we must be open to learning from any sort of interpretation at all. Do we really have to listen to or try to learn from conversation with racists and sexists, for example? Is there any way of precluding the necessity of these sorts of conversation from the start, of determining with whom we ought and with whom we ought not to talk or from whom we should and from whom we should not try to learn?

At first glance, Rawls's conception of an overlapping consensus might already appear to offer an answer to this question. Rawls denies that all versions of the good life will necessarily be able to thrive within a society in which the liberal conception of justice prevails. That conception is supported by a consensus of different philosophical, ethical and religious views although it derives from none of them and cannot be used to defend any one of them against the others. But even though the liberal conception of justice can be supported by all the comprehensive doctrines that can flourish in a liberal society, not all comprehensive doctrines can so flourish. If we concede, as Rawls does not, that different conceptions of the good can affect our interpretations of the meaning of principles of justice and other social norms, then it would seem that liberalism's own conception of justice might act as a brake on any dangerous plurality of interpretations. On this view, we need not worry about the impact of certain conceptions of the good on our understanding of the goods and traditions of a liberal order because the liberal conception of justice is not neutral in the respects that would be needed to allow such conceptions to thrive within it. Hence, we also need not worry that we might learn to revise our conception of justice to accord with what now seem to us to be morally objectionable interpretations of who we are. In a liberal regime the possibility of encountering these sorts of interpretation is minimized from the start.

This kind of limitation on the effects of an interpretive pluralism will not do for the purposes of providing for the rationality of hermeneutic conversation, however, because the limitation it provides is indiscriminate. The liberal conception of justice not only can exclude what seem now to members of a democratic society to be unworthy conceptions of the good but, as Rawls points out, it can exclude potentially "worthy" ones as well. The circumstance that an evaluative stance or a particular interpretation of our experience and traditions cannot flourish in a liberal regime furnishes no ground, then, for declaring base or irrational either it or the conceptions of justice that can issue from it. Were some of those interpretations to thrive, they might turn out to offer us an understanding of ourselves that was not only morally unobjectionable to us but a source of illumination for us. But if the standard of an overlapping consensus as the basis of support for our conceptions of justice cannot serve to define legitimate parameters for a *rational* hermeneutic conversation over our history, traditions and deepest political convictions, is there a standard that can?

Habermas's account of psychoanalytic theory is of interest in this regard for two reasons. First, it is meant to provide a way of discriminating between "undistorted" and "systematically distorted" communication and, hence, offers a proposal for just the parameters we are seeking. Second, it serves to describe a way in which our interpretive perspectives can be revised and transformed without their results requiring the universal assent of practical discourse. Examining Habermas's more detailed reflections on psychoanalysis, then, might help us to push his analyses of therapeutic and aesthetic critique further than he takes them in *The Theory of Communicative Action*. More importantly, it might help suggest a means of distinguishing rational hermeneutic conversation from its irrational counterpart.

Therapeutic Critique

As we saw in chapter 5, Habermas distinguishes therapeutic critique and aesthetic criticism from practical discourse on the basis of both the role of reasons within the former two and the scope of the agreement they can produce. The "unforced force" of good reasons can have only an indirect impact on our interpretations of our needs and interests and on our aesthetic evaluations because these are bound up with our cultural heritage, self-identity and values.

Although there may be good reasons for us to give up on the satisfaction of a particular need or interest, it is not clear that the force of reasons can extend to the way we simply understand the matters in question. We can come to understand both a work of art and ourselves differently than we have previously, but argumentation is not suited to effecting this transformation alône. Rather we have to come to read meaning in a different way, to understand the relevance of a different frame of reference to the work or life at issue and to connect up experiences in different ways. Others can point to factors of a work or of our own experience and traditions that might help us do this. But if we do not we are not necessarily just "wrong". Indeed, the question is, how might we assess the rationality of the change they ask of us? In other words, how do we differentiate, within hermeneutic conversation, between the potentially educational insights of others and systematic distortions in understanding and communication?

According to Habermas, strictly hermeneutic attempts to understand meaning are sufficient as long as the meanings that need to be understood are only temporarily incomprehensible and, indeed, are temporarily incomprehensible only because of their cultural, temporal or social distance from us. In such cases, even though we do not yet know how to understand the meanings at issue, we do know what kind of additional information we need in order to make them accessible. If we are trying to understand the meaning a particular social good had for the distant past of the society to which we belong, for example, we may be initially perplexed by the extent to which its former distribution deviates from our own arrangements for its distribution. Nevertheless, we do know how to proceed in order to understand this distribution. We know we need to understand the history and social context in which the good was a good, the other social meanings to which it was related, the social meanings to which it contrasts and the history of those meanings. We need to immerse ourselves as far as possible in the time period under study, to come to understand it as a second first language and participate in its language of action and practice.

Such a hermeneutic approach to understanding meaning is also sufficient, Habermas thinks, when "openly pathological" elements intrude upon the meanings to be understood. In this case, the interpreter of meaning can simply exclude those elements from his or her general interpretation much as we exclude from our interpretations aspects of a text that, from the perspective of our holistic understanding, seem simply misconceived. In both cases, we can develop a general interpretation of the text, social practice or life history and simply regard certain parts, actions or events as irrelevant to the overall meaning. That which concerns Habermas, however, is the intrusion of "patterns of systematically distorted communication" on to "pathologically unobtrusive speech." Here we cannot simply exclude pathological elements because they enter into and disrupt the very meaning we are trying to understand. The pathology does not cause any apparent incoherence that we might explicate. Still, to the extent that we continue to try to see the point or significance for us of the text or text analogue, as Gadamer's anticipation of completeness demands, we can also not comprehend the distortions it involves. As Habermas continues:

> Hermeneutics has taught us that we are always a participant as long as we move within the natural language ... There is therefore no general criterion available to us which would allow us to determine when we are subject to the false consensus of a pseudo-normal understanding and consider something as a difficulty that can be resolved by hermeneutic means when, in fact, it requires systematic explanation.[7]

I have stressed that a hermeneutic approach to the understanding of meaning can concede that we shall have to abandon our attempts to understand a text or text analogue if it appears incoherent or pointless even after serious attempts to grasp its meaning and truth for us. From within the parameters of a hermeneutic understanding, however, it seems that we can never know whether our failure to understand the text or text analogue in these cases is to be attributed to our failings as interpreters or to actual failings within that which we are trying to understand. As we saw, Taylor notes approvingly that there seems always to be a legitimate response to "I don't understand: namely change yourself." But, if we take this stance to all incomprehensible texts and interpretive perspectives, we also seem to risk changing where we should not, where the problem in understanding does not lie in us but in systematic distortions within that which we are trying to understand. Where we engage this meaning seriously, then, as the claims of hermeneutic conversation require, we seem to be in a situation analogous to that of a child who must take seriously the demands of a lunatic parent and even learn from them because, given the constraints of childhood dependency, he or she cannot understand that the parent is a lunatic. In doing so, what is achieved is not interpretive insight but, as Habermas puts it in another context, a "damaged life."[8] The same might be said for ideological interpretations of social meaning. Where we engage the meaning of *Plessy* seriously, as a coherent and best light interpretation of the equal protection clause, we simply miss its racism.

In Habermas's view, the only means of avoiding or overcoming the damaging effects of such influences is to take a more theoretical approach from the beginning. In the case of the "damaged life" of an individual, what is needed is a theory that includes a description of normal socialization processes, an analysis of the possible conditions that can cause deviations from it and an account of the general forms such deviations can take. Such a theory provides the framework within which the psychoanalyst attempts both to understand the real meaning of a patient's claims or actions and to help heal the distortions they involve. The same holds at the level of social meaning. We need a social theory that can identify the kinds of factors that can affect the self-understanding of a society and undermine the possibility of undistorted communication between social actors.

We saw in chapters 1 and 2 that both the German tradition of hermeneutics and neo-Wittgensteinian social science contend that we must always first understand the meaning of an action or practice before we can explain its causes. If we are trying to explain a behavior in terms of certain economic conditions, for example, we must understand that it is a behavior that can have an economic cause within the social and linguistic context of which it is a part and this means that we must first grasp its meaning in terms of the relevant framework of other social meanings. To be sure, we need not end our investigation with such an "internal" understanding. We need not understand a behavior only in the terms that the agents responsible for it understand it; it is certainly possible to understand a behavior in economic terms that the social agents themselves do not understand in this way. Still, both hermeneuticists and neo-Wittgensteinians argue that there must be some connection between the vocabulary that interpreters or social scientists use to articulate the meaning of the behavior and the language the social agents themselves use because the meaning of the behavior is in part constituted by its place in this language.[9]

Habermas argues that in coming to comprehend pathological symptoms analysts must reverse this approach. They cannot rely, even initially, on the meaning a patient's behavior may have within the language of action and practice of which it is a part because the point about this language is that it is deformed. The meaning the action has within it is not its meaning even for the patient; but because the patient also has no other language for articulating meaning, the behavior remains incomprehensible even to himself or herself. Rather than beginning with a contextual understanding of the meaning of the patient's expressions at all, then, the analyst must rely, from the very first, upon an explanatory theory that can rise above the restrictions of the deformed context itself to explain both the meaning of the behavior and the source of its specific incomprehensibility. As Habermas puts this point, "The what – the meaning-content of systematically distorted expressions – can only be 'understood' when it is possible to answer, at the same time, the 'why' question, i.e. to 'explain' the emergence of the symptomatic scene by reference to the initial conditions of the distortion itself."[10]

It bears reemphasizing that the problem with pathologically unobtrusive speech, for Habermas, is that it distorts a patient's self-understanding and self-presentation as a whole. A patient's symptomatic actions and expressions are not simply deviations from a more integrated self-interpretation; instead, they undermine the possibility of any non-pathological self-interpretation from the start. Because of pathological deformations within the language of understanding and interpretation itself, the possibility of a patient's revising his or her need and interest interpretations in a rational way requires a theoretically informed viewpoint. The patient cannot come to a better self-understanding through an internal dialogue since this dialogue will merely carry the original deformations of language with it. Nor can the patient come to a better self-understanding through the kind of discussion of interpretive and evaluative assessments we have identified with hermeneutic conversation, for these discussions can never penetrate to either the distorted character of the assessments or to its cause.

The same holds for the kind of internal criticism, ideas of reflective equilibrium or, indeed, hermeneutic conversation we have looked at on the social level. From Habermas's perspective, reliance on any of these hermeneutic forms of self-critique, self-justification and even self-transformation must simply reproduce any ideological distortions that exist in the original self-understanding of the society and its traditions. Hence, the possibility of either revising one's own social-political orientations and interpretations in a rational way or grasping the distortions in those of others requires a theoretically grounded approach. According to Habermas, it requires a critical theory of society that can combine the interpretive perspective of hermeneutics with a form of structural explanation and, by so doing, connect social meanings to the social and economic conditions that affect these meanings. As he writes, "Cultural tradition here loses the semblance of absolutism that a hermeneutics become autonomous had falsely claimed for it. Tradition can be accorded its place in the totality; it can be understood in its relation to the system of social labor and political domination."[11]

In Habermas's recent work, he elaborates this explanatory framework in a way informed by systems theory. For the purposes of the question we are examining in this chapter, however, the specifics of Habermas's critical theory are not as important as the strategy it employs, that of supplementing hermeneutic insight into meaning with a theoretically informed account of the conditions and genesis of that meaning. As in the case of psychoanalytic theory, what is important about this theoretical approach is that it is characterized by the reversal of the hermeneutic primacy of understanding meaning over structural explanation so that the meanings to be understood − for example the meaning of certain policies and compromises within contemporary welfare states − are first identified within a theoretical framework. This reversal involves, first, a theoretical account not only of individual socialization processes, as in psychoanalytic theory but, more generally, of processes of social reproduction and the transmission of cultural knowledge as well; second, it involves a theoretical account of the possible causes and structure of deviation from the theoretical model; and finally, it thereby allows for the specification of probable points of social crisis or disruption as the notion of an Oedipus crisis does in individual socialization.

Habermas's theoretical analysis constitutes only one possible approach to the critique of ideology, of course. Foucault's genealogical investigations are another and I have focused on Habermas's work here only because it takes off directly from the Gadamerian hermeneutics I used in the last chapter to help generate the conception of hermeneutic conversation. If we limit our discussion to Habermas's work, however, a hermeneutic perspective gives rise to a question of its own: namely, what is meant to secure the objectivity of a critical theory itself? If the definitive characteristic of a critical theory is its reversal of understanding and explanation, what kind of explanation is this and what guarantees its comprehensiveness as against the inevitable partiality of interpretation? Why are the claims of psychoanalysis, for example, not to be considered simply particular interpretations of childhood socialization processes, interpretations, moreover, that are skewed in an offensively sexist way? How can any critical social theory, whether Habermasian or not, help set parameters for interpretive conversations? They would rather seem to have to be part of such conversations themselves, some of the inevitably partial interpretations entered into the conversation for purposes of mutual insight. Habermas's answer to this sort of conclusion is to appeal to the character of a reconstructive science.

Reconstructive Sciences and Hermeneutic Conversation

Habermas contends that a hermeneutic understanding of meaning involves interpreting the content of a text or text analogue, investigating the connections between meanings and attempting to link what he calls the "surface-structure" of incomprehensible "formations" with the surface structure of more familiar "formations."[12] Hermeneutic understanding thus involves capacities for paraphrasing expressions, articulating the meaning of actions and practices and translating expressions from one language into those of another. Reconstructive sciences, in contrast, are concerned with deep structures, with the rules behind the generation of the actions and expressions themselves. They do not attempt to articulate an originally unclear meaning, whether that of a text or that of such text analogues as actions, practices and social goods. Rather, they attempt to render explicit the intuitive knowledge and abilities of acting and speaking subjects, to go below the formations of sentences, utterances and actions to the understanding of rules or know-how that makes them possible. As Habermas writes, "The object of understanding is no longer the content of a symbolic expression or what specific authors meant by it in specific situations but the intuitive rule consciousness that a competent speaker has of his own language."[13]

Where this reconstructed "intuitive rule consciousness" reflects a universal knowledge or capacity, "a general cognitive, linguistic or interactive competence," reconstructive sciences make explicit what Habermas calls "species competences"[14] and it is for this reason that they can claim the status of theoretical knowledge. He cites as examples such disciplines as logic and meta-mathematics, epistemology, the philosophy of science, Chomskian linguistics, Kohlbergian ethics, action theory and the theory of argumentation.

> Common to all these disciplines is the goal of providing an account of the pretheoretical knowledge and the intuitive command of rule systems that underlie the production and evaluation of such symbolic expressions and achievements as correct inferences; good arguments; accurate descriptions, explanations, and predictions; grammatically correct sentences; successful speech acts; effective instrumental action; appropriate evaluations; authentic self-presentations; etc.[15]

What all these disciplines aim to show are the inescapable presuppositions of entering into the relevant practices or, as Habermas puts it, "the general and necessary conditions for the validity of symbolic expressions and achievements."[16]

Reconstructive sciences differ from empirical-analytic sciences in four respects. First, the data for reconstructive sciences is not supplied by observation as it is in the explanatory sciences. Rather, for purposes of forming and testing hypotheses, reconstructive sciences must look to the rule-consciousness of competent speakers and actors, in the case of a generative linguistics, for example, to their intuitive knowledge of how to generate grammatical sentences. But the inquirer's knowledge of this rule consciousness must therefore be obtained through a "maeutic" process in which he or she draws out the intuitive "know-how" of competent subjects by questioning them in various ways and providing suitable examples or counter-examples. Second, the relation of reconstructive theory to its object domain differs from the relation of empirical theories to theirs. Reconstructive sciences do not try to explain phenomena with the aid of nomological hypotheses; they rather serve to explicate an intuitive knowledge and their relation to their object domain is thus more that of explicans to explicandum than that of explanans to explanandum. This means, third, that reconstructive sciences cannot replace an everyday account of a capacity with a scientific one and, fourth, that although reconstructive hypotheses can represent the pre-theoretical knowledge of competent speakers and actors more or less adequately, they cannot falsify it. "At most, the report of a speaker's intuition can prove to be false, but not the intuition itself. The latter belongs to the data and the data can be explained but not criticized."[17]

Still, reconstructive sciences are similar to empirical-analytic sciences both in their universal scope and inasmuch as their research hypotheses must be empirically verified. Habermas avoids using a transcendental terminology to describe the notion of unavoidable presuppositions reconstructions involve. "There is always the possibility that they rest on a false choice of examples, that they are obscuring and distorting correct intuitions, or, even more frequently, that they are overgeneralizing individual cases." Neverthless, while reconstructive sciences are thus fallible and in need of "further corroboration," Habermas does not consider them inevitably partial as hermeneutic interpretations are. Although "critique of all a priori and strong transcendental claims is certainly justified," he writes, "it should not discourage attempts to put rational reconstructions of presumably basic competences to the test, subjecting them to indirect verification by using them as inputs in empirical theories."[18]

To the extent that such reconstructions explicate the "conditions for the validity of symbolic expressions and achievements," they also serve to illuminate deviations from such "communicative competence" and to provide the framework for the explanation of such deviations. To this extent, reconstructions also serve a critical function. They provide standards for the validity of communicative agreements and help specify the conditions that can lead to communicative failures or disturbances. The question now is whether such critical standards can resolve the problem with which we are concerned as to the rationality of specifically hermeneutic conversation. In other words, suppose we take up Habermas's claims both about the necessity of a systematic and explanatory approach to uncovering ideological distortions in communication and about the reconstructive foundation of these approaches. How do these claims affect the conditions of legitimacy or rationality for the specifically hermeneutic discussion of what our history and experience means, who we are and what principles of justice are appropriate for us?

In chapter 5, I criticized Habermas's implicit attempt simply to subsume this kind of discussion under the logic of practical discourse and to require a universal rational consensus from it. As elaborated in chapter 6, the aim of hermeneutic discussion is not necessarily a consensus over social meaning any more than the aim of a discussion of interpretations of *Hamlet* is complete agreement over the text. We are concerned, instead, to expand and develop the interpretations we favor, to learn from other interpretations and to gain new insights into the dimensions of meaning a text or text analogue possesses. Just as we would not want to claim that my understanding of myself must be approved by a universal consensus, we do not want to say that any interpretation of meaning must be acceptable to all under certain ideal conditions. Instead, the question of the meaning of American involvement in Vietnam, for example, is a complex and multidimensional one for which no one understanding can be canonical. At the same time, we seem to need some rational boundaries within which understandings can be considered acceptable. Otherwise we shall have to consider seriously, as sources of possible insight, not only lunatic answers, no matter how apparently constrained in Dworkin's sense, but responses that are racist, sexist and so on. What further constraints, then, can be placed on this kind of hermeneutic discussion from the vantage point of a theoretical approach to ideology?

If we start with this quite unHabermasian idea of a hermeneutic conversation as the means through which a society develops its self-understanding in a pluralistic way, then Habermas's version of a critical theory of society can be applied in such a way that it asks us to attend to two circumstances. First, our continuing attempts to understand ourselves and our history may always proceed under conditions affected, not only by mutually enlightening hermeneutic conversation, but by social and economic conditions and relations of power that intrude upon and distort that conversation. Second, these same external factors mean that there may always be voices and interpretations that have been systematically left out of a society's interpretive conversations from the start.

The workers whom Walzer cites who are trying to understand what the principle of equality means for them can serve as examples of the first circumstance. In opposition to Marx, Walzer claims that these workers cannot be accused of possessing "false consciousness" because it may be that, for them, "the equality realized in capitalist society is genuine equality or equality enough."[19] But what is the status of this interpretation if it is one generated not as much by the workers' own experiences and understanding as by its status as a dominant interpretation, one backed by the support of those either in power or advantaged by the existing social and economic conditions? What if other interpretations of the meaning of equality, ones in which workers might learn to find more of their needs reflected, are censored either by state power or economic considerations? It may be that we can no longer talk of false consciousness if we give up on finding uniquely true interpretations of specific meanings. But, by the same token, we cannot just assume that the "equality realized in capitalist society is ... equality enough" if alternative interpretive options do not have the same social and economic clout, publicity, access to media and so forth.

As an example of the second circumstance that interpreters of social meaning need to note, namely, the potential exclusion of certain groups from a society's self-interpretive discussions, we might look once again at the *Plessy v. Ferguson* decision, for it can be argued that what makes this decision peculiar is precisely that it dismisses the interpretive assessment of one of the very groups it affects. One of the rationales for the decision was that the slight to blacks involved in Jim Crow laws was simply self-created; the laws were not intended to disadvantage or denigrate blacks, but simply to provide separate but equal facilities for them. But if we are to take the idea of a hermeneutic conversation seriously, the discussion cannot end with these claims. Instead, we need to hear from the affected group as to why it interprets the laws as it does and we need to presume the validity of this interpretation. Moreover, we need to investigate the social conditions under which this interpretation is given such short shrift.

In order further to clarify this combination of critical and interpretive approaches within hermeneutic conversation, we can turn to a recent discussion of "the politics of need interpretation" in Nancy Fraser's "Struggle over Needs: Outline of a Socialist-Feminist Critical Theory of Late Capitalist Political Culture."[20] In a sense, this discussion brings us full circle since it again focuses on the understanding of social needs with which we began both our discussion of Walzer's work and our examination of the problems of interpretive conflict and rationality that follow from the hermeneutic turn. In exploring Fraser's essay I have two purposes: first, to present a concrete instance of a Habermasian approach to interpretive problems and, second, to push that approach in a more hermeneutic direction.

The Politics of Need Interpretation

By "the politics of need interpretation," Fraser means different things at different times and she sometimes shies away from the issues on which we have focused in this book. That is, she often seems to skim over those dimensions of need interpretation involving the questions of whether a particular social good is a social need and how, if so, it is to be defined. Instead, she conflates these questions with the question of how different social groups think a given social need should be satisfied. Nonetheless, where she does separate out the issue of understanding the meanings of a social good, Fraser offers an important corrective to the ideal model we gave of hermeneutic conversation in chapter 6. She begins with the salutary recognition that what she calls late capitalist societies are not simply pluralistic; they are rather stratified along lines of class, sex, race and ethnic heritage and, moreover, divided into social groups with unequal status, power and access to media of communication. Under these conditions, certain groups have an easier time establishing the cogency of their interpretations of social goods than others. As Fraser puts the point, "*who* gets to establish authoritative thick definitions of people's needs is itself a political stake"[21] and it is a political stake of crucial significance for any attempt to defend an interpretive pluralism.

Any society, according to Fraser, involves certain "sociocultural means of interpretation and communication" or "discursive resources." In socially and economically stratified societies these means are themselves diverse, a "polyglot field of ... possibilities and alternatives" and we must therefore distinguish those "that are hegemonic, authorized and officially sanctioned, on the one hand, from those that are nonhegemonic, disqualified, and discounted, on the other hand."[22] While certain means of interpretation and communication have an established place in the institutions of the society, in the university discourse, the courts of law, the media and the domains of government, others are "enclaved" in what Fraser calls "subcultural sociolects" that are excluded from the more official interpretive arenas. For this reason, "needs talk appears as a site of struggle where groups with unequal discursive (and nondiscursive) resources compete to establish as hegemonic their respective interpretations of legitimate social needs."[23]

Fraser's discussion of wife-battering is a case in point. She distinguishes three moments in the struggle over needs: "the struggle to establish or deny the political status of a given need," "the struggle for the power to define it" and "the struggle over the satisfaction of the need."[24] From our hermeneutic perspective, it is not clear that the first two of these moments can be analytically distinguished since the definition of what a particular need is would seem to serve already to establish or deny its political status. At one time wife-battering was conceived of as wife-beating, by which was meant that it was a purely private and domestic affair similar to the disciplining of children. Correspondingly, the needs of women who were beaten were considered matters concerning their own choices and actions. If there were considered to be "needs" involved at all these were seen for the most part as individual needs to make other choices or even to act in a way not deserving of "punishment." The struggle to bring wife-beating into the open and to provoke a social understanding of the need for protection was, then, largely a struggle to define the practice, to allow it to be viewed not as a deserved punishment or an individual problem but as wife-battering and, thus, as a social disease. As Fraser herself writes, "Feminist activists renamed the practice with a term drawn from criminal law ... its etiology was not to be traced to individual women's or men's emotional problems but, rather, to the ways these problems refracted pervasive social relations of male dominance and female subordination."[25]

The point here is that an interpretation of a practice will serve to define both what the need is that it involves and whether that need is considered a social one, one that the society must undertake to satisfy for its members, at whatever level. For precisely this reason, it matters which groups in the society can offer privileged interpretations of social meanings. "Dominant groups," Fraser writes, "articulate need interpretations intended to exclude, defuse and/or co-opt counterinterpretations. Subordinate or oppositional groups, on the other hand, articulate need interpretations intended to challenge, displace, and/or modify dominant ones."[26] In the case of battered women, feminists, as an oppositional group, were largely successful in modifying a socially entrenched interpretation of wifebeating and thereby in gaining public recognition of a formerly hidden need.

What are we to make of this success? Fraser points out that the victory was not without its costs. The public recognition of the needs of battered women meant that women's shelters not only finally received public funding but were, in addition, subjected to certain administrative regulations, accounting procedures and accreditation requirements that changed their nature. Whereas they began as shelters offered to battered women by feminists and once-battered women themselves, they became shelters run by a professional staff. The consequence has been that the needs of the women involved are interpreted more in therapeutic than political terms, as needs for higher self-esteem and consciousness-raising rather than for social and economic independence. The struggle over the interpretation of the meaning of the need thus continues. It has simply changed from a debate over the meaning of a particular action or practice to one over the concrete or "thick" meaning of the need to which the actions are commonly understood to give rise. But how are we to view the different voices in this debate?

Fraser concludes her essay with a criticism of the relativistic leanings of certain feminist positions. "To say that needs are culturally constructed and discursively interpreted is not to say that any need interpretation is as good as any other."[27] The debate over wife-battering as opposed to wife-beating seems to be ended since there seem to be few members of modern Western societies, anyway, who can stomach the conception of women that sanctioning or ignoring such abuse as a purely private matter requires. But, do we attempt to legitimate one interpretation of the needs of battered women over another, once we understand them as battered women? Fraser offers the following two-part schema for adjudicating between different interpretations of needs:

> First, there are procedural considerations concerning the social processes by which various competing need interpretations are generated. For example, how exclusive or inclusive are various rival needs discourses? How hierarchical or egalitarian are the relations among the interlocutors? In general, procedural considerations dictate that, all other things being equal, the best need interpretations are those reached by means of communicative processes that most closely approximate ideals of democracy, equality and fairness.
>
> In addition, considerations of consequences are relevant in justifying need interpretations. This means comparing alternative distributive out-

comes of rival interpretations. For example, would widespread acceptance of some given interpretation of a social need disadvantage some
groups of people vis-a-vis others? Does the interpretation conform to,
rather than challenge, societal patterns of dominance and subordination? Are the rival chains of in-order-to relations to which competing
need interpretations belong more or less respectful, as opposed to
transgressive, of ideological boundaries that delimit "separate spheres"
and thereby rationalize inequality? In general, consequentialist considerations dictate that, all other things being equal, the best need interpretations are those that do not disadvantage some groups of people
vis-à-vis others.[28]

How is this schema to be applied to the conflict between wife-
battering and wife-beating interpretations of a practice? On the
procedural side, feminists try to articulate and press the needs of
abused women, thereby rectifying an imbalance in the relations between an ignored and oppositional mode of interpretation, on the
one hand, and an entrenched one, on the other. From a consequentialist point of view, feminists ask which interpretation is least likely
to disadvantage one group of people against others and answer
this question in favor of the interpretation of wife-battering. In this
instance, the interpretations of other social groups attempting to
privatize the meaning of both the practice and the need are simply
not convincing because they allow for a continuation of the abuse.
To this argument, it might of course be replied that the men putting up with disobedient, slovenly and incompetent wives are the
real sufferers and that we should just as well listen to and advocate
their position. But here, Fraser would presumably recur to the procedural considerations: Is this an analysis that could be reached in a
communicative process approximating ideals of democracy, equality and fairness?

Reached by whom? we might ask. These procedural considerations bring us close to the model of a consensus under conditions
of ideal speech, a model I tried to reject in chapter 5. Before tack-
ling this problem, however, we might ask how Fraser's schema is
to be applied to the second case of interpretive conflict that her
discussion treats, namely that between therapeutic and political definitions of battered women's needs. Fraser clearly assumes the
greater strength of the feminist, political position in this case. But
here, I think, is an instance in which her analysis might be pushed
in the more pluralistic direction that the idea of hermeneutic conversation takes. The question that clearly arises is why we need to
pick between these two interpretations at all. Indeed, it would
seem that battered women benefit from both, that the problem of

wife-battering is both a personal problem of low self-esteem and a social problem of female economic dependence and male oppression. Hence, it is crucial that both interpretations be given a voice. Are the relations between the two "needs discourses" hierarchical? Does either "disadvantage some groups of people vis-à-vis others"? The answer to both questions seems to be "no" as long as both interpretations remain available to the battered women themselves. In Fraser's view, depriving battered women of a political analysis of their situation in favor of a therapeutic one does disadvantage them and she offers compelling examples of the way various groups of women have resisted the interpretive reduction of their circumstances to ones of low self-esteem. Still, with regard to the second question, we might argue that depriving battered women either of political interpretations of their situation or of therapy would be to disadvantage them and that neither excludes the other.

Can such a pluralistic conception be applied to the first case in which we are considering alternative understandings of a practice as either wife-beating or wife-battering? Can we allow it to be understood in both ways or do we have to reject the second interpretation on procedural grounds, as Fraser seems to assume, as unlikely to be reached in a democratic, fair and equal communicative process? In my view, the problem with the way in which Fraser appeals to procedural grounds is that it anticipates a consensus in interpretation; it assumes that a justified interpretation is one likely to be agreed upon or "reached" on Habermasian foundations or "in a communicative process approximating ideals of democracy, equality, and fairness." But, from a hermeneutic point of view, there is no reason either to expect a unitary interpretation of any meaning, whether social or textual, or to want one. Fraser claims she does not "think that justification can be understood in traditional objectivist terms as correspondence, as if it were a matter of finding the interpretation that matches the true nature of the need as it really is in itself..." Nor does she take the traditional Marxist line according to which justifying an interpretation is "a matter of finding the one group in society with the privileged 'standpoint.'"[29] Still, to the extent that discourse approximating Habermas's ideal conditions is meant to produce a consensus over interpreted meaning, it precludes diversity. From a hermeneutic point of view, not only is there no "right" interpretation in either of the senses that Fraser dismisses, there is no uniquely right interpretation on procedural grounds either and to look for or to anticipate one is to overlook the possibilities for continuing self-education we can derive from a plurality of interpretations.

Obviously we might ask at this point what possible education we can receive from a sexist or "suffering male" interpretation of the practice of wife-beating. This is the kind of question with which we began this chapter. But if we reject the suffering male interpretation on procedural grounds, we do not have to reject the possibility that different interpretations might be legitimately reached by different groups in a communicative process approximating the ideals of democracy, equality and fairness. Moreover, if most of us do reject the interpretation of wife-beating in favor of wife-battering it is not simply because feminists have corrected a procedural imbalance in the equality of competing interpretations. We reject it also because feminists have managed to educate us, because they have made it clear to us what our understanding of ourselves as members of a certain kind of society requires of us. To this extent, it makes sense to understand the procedural parameters of fairness, equality and democracy as necessary conditions of hermeneutic discussion; they can be considered means of clearing the ground for a hermeneutic conversation over constrained interpretations in Dworkin's sense or the means by which we can try to guarantee a level playing field for all the competing interpretations. Still, they can themselves neither guarantee a consensus over meaning nor themselves define the educational or compelling force of particular interpretations. At this point, education is rather of the illuminative sort suggested by Habermas's account of aesthetic criticism; it is a matter of reacting to things differently, and of understanding and being affected by meaning differently than we were before.

Fraser misconstrues the point of her two-part schema insofar as she sees it as one involved in justifying certain interpretations over others. Under the notion of hermeneutic conversation I have tried to promote, the schema would have to be understood as a means simply of clearing the ground or leveling the playing ground for an interpretive discussion between all interested parties but it is not the place of political theory, itself, to decide which interpretations are better than which others. The role of political theory would seem rather to be threefold: insisting upon the fairness of the debate among different interpretations, uncovering the concrete social and economic factors militating against a fair, equal and democratic discussion and helping to articulate those interpretive perspectives to which the institutions and structures of the society as it stands do not give voice. Sometimes these new voices appear to be so compelling that competing interpretations simply die out on their own. This appears to be the case in the discussion of how wife beating or battering is to be defined. Even in this case, however, the interpretive point is not adequately conceptualized as one of a consensus over the right interpretation guaranteed on both procedural and consequentialist grounds. Rather, feminist criticism gives voice to an alternative interpretation, overcomes the social and economic barriers that make the society deaf to this interpretation and educates the society to which it belongs.

If we accept the appeal to procedural grounds, now not as a substitute for hermeneutic conversation and mutual education, but rather as a means of securing a level playing field, on what do we base these procedural grounds? For what reasons and, indeed, for what society can we appeal to the standards of fairness, equality and democracy? This is the point at which Richard Rorty, following what might be called a traditional hermeneutic conception, parts company with Habermas. Habermas, of course, appeals to the principles of a communicative rationality that emerge from a rational reconstruction of the pragmatic structures of communication oriented to understanding:

> A critically enlightened hermeneutics that differentiates between insight and illusion incorporates the metahermeneutic awareness of the conditions of the possibility of systematically distorted communication. It connects the process of understanding to the principle of rational discourse according to which truth would be guaranteed only by that kind of consensus which was achieved under the idealized conditions of unconstrained communication free from domination and which could be maintained over time.[30]

But Rorty claims that this appeal is an instance of "scratching where it does not itch."[31] If we are concerned with the means of correcting imbalances in communication and overcoming systematic distortions, these means remain grounded only in the traditions of a democratic society. Indeed, standards for undistorted communication can refer only to *"our* criteria of relevance, where we are the people who have read and pondered Plato, Newton, Kant, Marx, Darwin, Freud, Dewey etc."[32] The implications of Rorty's view for any idea of hermeneutic conversation are clearly relativistic. If we claim that the criteria of democracy, equality and fairness are simply the criteria of relevance we use for leveling the playing field on which interpretations are to compete, then we also have to assume that those who reject these criteria might have a point. Indeed, we have to assume that our task as interpreters is to understand the point in this rejection and to learn from it.

For her part, Fraser takes a middle position. She claims that she does not want to follow Habermas in grounding her schema "in the conditions of possibility of speech understood universalistically and ahistorically;" it rather represents "a contingently evolved, historically specific possibility."[33] In other words, the procedural grounds to which we are to appeal are both "our criteria of relevance" as members of democratic societies and criteria the possibility of which depends upon a historical process. But it seems to me that once we shift the emphasis to hermeneutic conversation we can also generate the fair, equal and democratic grounds on which hermeneutic conversation is to proceed out of the requirements of hermeneutic conversation itself. The idea behind the notion of hermeneutic conversation is the idea that an interpretive pluralism can be educational for all the parties involved. If we are to be educated by interpretations other than our own, however, we must both encourage the articulation of those alternative interpretations and help to make them as compelling as they can be. And how can we do this except by assuring the fairness of the conversation and working to give all possible voices equal access? If we are to learn from our hermeneutic efforts, then no voice can retain a monopoly on interpretation and no voice can try to limit in advance what we might learn from others. Democracy thus turns out to be the condition for the possibility of an enriching exchange of insight. Democratic conditions act against the entrenchment of bigoted interpretations by offering others a fair fight as equals and hermeneutic conversation itself acts against the reduction of diversity by allowing that more than one rational interpretation might "win."

In this way, it seems to me that Habermasian ideas can be made fruitful for a very unHabermasian conception of discourse. What we take from Habermas, and from the critique of ideology in general, is the awareness of systematic disturbances in communication caused by social and economic conditions. We also take the idea of a discussion in which all voices are given equal time, play and attention. We understand these democratic standards both as rooted in historical possibilities and as crucial to the self-educational possibilities of hermeneutic conversation. The aim of this sort of discussion is neither solely a consensus over norms nor even solely an agreement over meaning. It is rather the kind of mutual education that goes on in the humanities and for which insight, enrichment and development, not canonical understandings, are the goal.

8

CONCLUSION

The interpretive turn in political philosophy abandons the attempt to ground universally valid principles of justice in features of human action or rational choice and attempts, instead, to articulate those principles of justice that are suitable for a particular culture and society because of that culture's and society's traditions, the meanings of its social goods and its public values. Once, however, this interpretive analysis is substituted for a more universalistic and foundationalist approach, problems of interpretive conflict also seem to arise. Even if the meanings of a society's goods, needs, practices and traditions are "social constructions," different groups within the society can interpret these meanings and traditions in different ways. How might a society adjudicate, then, between these different ways in order to come to an agreement on the principles of justice and, indeed, on the actions and practices appropriate for it?

We can appeal to traditional hermeneutic standards of coherence to reject interpretations that fail to make any sense at all out of the meanings at issue. Hence, we might reject an interpretation of American health care practices that claimed that health and longevity had no meaning as needs for the society at all even if we do not consider their meaning as needs to be exhaustive of all dimensions of their meaning. To claim health is not a need at all for the society simply fails to fit the evidence or makes a "shambles" of what it is supposed to understand, to use Dworkin's word. Nevertheless, there remain conflicts between different interpretations of meaning that fit equally well: between two interpretations of the role of the need aspect of medical care, for example, or the needs of battered women. We can add to the standard of fit Dworkin's standard of "best light" according to which an interpretation must make of a text or text analogue the best it can be. Still, we must then face the problem of conflicts over which interpretation does conceive of a particular text or text analogue in its best light and what constitutes the standard of best light itself. Rorty's interpretation of the meaning of the Vietnam War according to which it violated America's own hopes, ideals and self-image is a best light interpretation of those hopes, ideals and self-image from the point of view of certain commitments Rorty holds. A different best light interpretation might emphasize different hopes, ideals and a different self-image.

Given this pluralism in the understandings different groups can have of their culture's political traditions, we might claim that we need to find institutional solutions that can be "faithful" to all the differences. In this regard, Taylor's idea of simply accommodating different interpretive stances seems promising and Walzer mentions a similar idea in a parenthesis in *Spheres of Justice*: "When people disagree about the meaning of social goods, when understandings are controversial, then justice requires that the society be faithful to the disagreements, providing institutional channels for their expression, adjudicative mechanisms, and alternative distributions."[1] Neither Taylor nor Walzer considers how this might be done concretely, however. Nor is it clear how it could be done when we disagree not only over the meaning of our tradition as a whole but the meaning of individual goods and actions. Hence, while we might look for ways of accommodating both Lockean and Rousseauian elements in our tradition as a whole, it is not clear how we are to accommodate different understandings of the meaning of medical care, specifically, or the meaning of American intervention in foreign disputes. Finally, the idea of accommodation does not seem particularly resolute when we may be dealing, not with a simple plurality of interpretations, but with certain interpretations that are either ideological or pathological. The problem here is that there may be paranoid interpretations of an action or interpretations of meanings and traditions that rest on other systematic distortions. These interpretations may be internally coherent and they may seem to their interpreters to constitute best light interpretations in the sense that they make the text or text analogue at issue the best it can be from their skewed point of view. Still, the interpretations may be so insane and monolithically constructed – interpretations of American history offered by the Ku Klux Klan are a case in point here – that no strictly interpretive attempt to exhibit their internal contradictions seems to be able to penetrate them.

MacIntyre contends that the idea of accommodation indicates just how barren the tradition of liberal individualism is. We need to accommodate different interpretations of our traditions, in his view, only because we have given up on the truth of any of them. If, instead, we take up a conception of rationality as embedded in traditions, we can require that different conceptions of the good and the different conceptions of justice that follow from them justify themselves in conversation with one another. In so doing we can forge a kind of open-ended but Hegelian synthesis in which we retain those aspects of our views that withstand criticism and dispense with those that cannot. In chapter 6 I tried to suggest that this idea of justificatory conversation is necessary to a hermeneutic approach. The idea of synthesis is not, however; at least a hermeneutic approach will have to allow that different groups and different traditions will be able to infer different syntheses from their conversation with one another. Conversation is important to a hermeneutic approach to questions of justice not because it leads necessarily to one rationally justified synthesis but because the attempt to justify one's interpretations to others allows reform and revision of own interpretations. We can come to recognize the insights of others and try to incorporate them into our own view; furthermore, we can recognize the substantive dangers our interpretation risks and try to develop it in such a way as to avoid them. In the end, hermeneutic conversation allows us to intervene in the political practice of our community with an understanding of it and its history that is both as adequate as we can make it at the time and open to self-revision. Since, we recognize that it remains only an interpretation, we are also open to any illumination we can cull from others.

Does the rationality of hermeneutic conversation require more? I have suggested that it does, for if we allow for systematically distorted interpretations of meaning, such as those offered of American history by the Ku Klux Klan, we cannot assume that all interpretive conversations will be equally educational. What are the interpretive insights to be drawn from conversations in which one party has more power than another or less compunction about resorting to violence, in which the external constraints of money and social domination impede the free exchange and development of ideas or in which widespread and dominant beliefs about the status of one's sex or race distort the articulation of one's own need and interest interpretations? Because these are cases in which conversation is more likely to have ideological than educational effects, Habermas, Rorty and Fraser all appeal to an ideal of unconstrained communication. As applied to hermeneutic conversation, such an ideal means that only those interpretive conversations can be assumed to be rational and productive that are fair and democratic and that allow for the equality of the interpreters.

For Rorty, this ideal is simply the ideal of liberal politics and refers simply to values embedded in a democratic tradition itself. But we could not adopt this account of the ideal while retaining the hermeneutic "anticipation" of reciprocal education through conversation. To do so, we would have to assume that those who rejected the ideal might have a point and that our task as interpreters was to make sense of their rejection. Hence, if the Ku Klux Klan not only offers an insane picture of America but refuses to listen to any other interpretation on the grounds that democracy is a sin against the superiority of the white race, it becomes incumbent upon us, as interpreters, to try to make sense out of this idea. Habermas grounds the ideal of unconstrained communication, instead, on reconstructive sciences, and thus tries to escape this sort of predicament. Whatever the problems with this program, it could be plausibly argued that replacing Kantian political theory with the diversity of possible interpretations of meaning remains a frightening prospect. It can be made less frightening only by combining hermeneutic conversation with close attention to the possibility of systematic disturbances and imbalances in hermeneutic conversation itself. But this kind of attention is part of hermeneutic conversation itself, for if such conversation is meant to be mutually educational then it requires fairness and equality of itself.

Consensus, however, need not be the only goal of either politics or political theory any more than it is of literary criticism. To be sure, any society will have to decide on some principles of justice, sustain or develop some institutions and pursue some specific practices. But it is not clear that the task of political philosophy is to decide just what these are. Its task may be, instead, to establish the conditions in the society for fair, equal and democratic self-interpretive discussions and, correlatively, to investigate the social conditions of power and domination that impede them. Political philosophy may not be able to provide for consensual solutions to contemporary social issues. Still, it can investigate the social impediments to a fair and equal discussion among the members of the community and, by doing so, it can try to provide for a continuing and rational hermeneutic conversation. Moreover, while we may not be able to guarantee that all its interpretive voices will always be adequately represented or accommodated in a democratic society's practices and institutional arrangements at any given time, the idea of hermeneutic conversation can make two requests. First, assuming that the self-interpretive discussion of the society proceeds on a fair and inclusive basis, as far as possible, these arrangements should reflect the society's different understandings of its shared goods, historical traditions and political convictions. Second, where this kind of representation is not possible, where any action requires an exclusion of some interpretations, we need to recognize both this exclusion and the possibility of change. In this way, by recognizing that all interpretations are not simply fallible but also partial, we try to provide for a continuing conversation in which different voices can be heard, in which their insights can be taken seriously and in which our aspiration remains that of learning from these insights to develop a richer, more differentiated understanding of ourselves and our history.

The controversy over abortion in the United States offers an interesting test case for this ideal of a rational hermeneutic conversation. There are two aspects of this case that are noteworthy for our purposes. First, the *Roe v. Wade* decision that declared abortion to be a constitutionally protected right did nothing to settle the debate. Although there may be only one school in the legal domain to which attendance is mandatory, as Fiss insists, nonetheless the opinions of the US Supreme Court do not replace processes of debate and decision-making in a democratic society. Second, the character of this debate is less than rational. Hysteria about aborting fetuses is met with hysteria about women's lives; talk of denying the rights of the unborn is met with talk of denying the rights of mothers; pro-life advocates are thought to be ignorant and superstitious while pro-choice advocates are thought to be mass murderers.

What can the notion of hermeneutic conversation add to this controversy? It can help clarify the subject matter of the debate by shifting the emphasis from a conflict between two opposing rights, those of fetuses and those of women, to a conflict between two interpretations of the actions and practices that are consonant with American traditions and self-understandings. The controversy will no longer be considered as one over correct principles. To use Dworkin's terminology, it will now be one, instead, over the resolution appropriate to the United States as a community of integrity. The effect of this change is already to soften the opposition since it can no longer be conceived of as an opposition between the forces of good and the forces of evil. It is rather a controversy over the way in which the society can best understand and define itself.

But, of course, there may be at least two opposing conceptions of just how it can best understand and define itself. For the pro-life position, banning all abortions may be the only action consistent both with a history of expanding the domain of protected rights and with the idea of the United States as an ethical community or as the protector of the defenseless. For the pro-choice position, protecting the possibility of abortion as a constitutional right may be the only action consistent, again, with the expansion of the domain of rights and with the idea of the United States as a land of equality and opportunity. We cannot both ban abortions and protect the right to them. But we can recognize that each of the positions on abortion might learn from the other once we acknowledge that neither one has an exclusive grasp on either correct principles or social meaning. Indeed, it seems plausible to suggest that an extensive hermeneutically oriented debate over abortion might lead Americans to a consensus over somewhat of a middle position. Such a consensus would be the result, not of a bitter compromise but of a genuine education on both sides. Even without such a consensus, progress can be made by recasting the character of the debate as one over the diverse meanings of a political and ethical tradition as opposed to one over moral, religious or philosophical truth. Progress here means an increased tolerance and respect for each other but it also means the possibility of changing and developing oneself.

But suppose we now apply the procedural and consequentialist criteria to which Fraser points us. Procedural considerations dictate that the best interpretations are those reached by means of communicative processes that most closely approximate ideals of democracy, equality and fairness. First, then, can we eliminate either the pro-life or the pro-choice position by considering the social processes by which the competing interpretations are generated? How exclusive or inclusive are the rival discourses? How hierarchical or egalitarian are the relations among the interlocutors? Here, the answer seems to be that neither interpretation includes or excludes more than the other. The pro-life position excludes women as people who must be able to determine their lives for themselves while the pro-choice position eliminates fetuses. Moreover, we might say both interpretations involve or are generated by competing conceptions of the good and that neither needs to be constructed hierarchically or take a hierarchical attitude to the other.

Fraser's consequentialist considerations dictate that the best interpretations are those that do not disadvantage some groups of people vis-à-vis others. Second, then, can we eliminate either of the positions by comparing their results? Would widespread acceptance of a pro-life interpretation disadvantage women vis-à-vis others? Obviously, yes. Would widespread acceptance of a pro-choice interpretation disadvantage fetuses vis-à-vis others? Again, yes, although in this case it is not clear that being the unwanted child of a young teenager is not also a disadvantage vis-à-vis others. Neither side seems better or worse on procedural and consequentialist grounds; rather, the issues here dictate that the different sides will apply procedural and consequentialist criteria in different ways and to different parts of the subject matter. As I said in the last chapter, then, these criteria are relevant to assessing the fairness of a conversation, to assuring the even character of the playing field. But procedural and consequentialist considerations do not themselves decide the debate. To be sure, some pro-life advocates are simply sexist; nonetheless a quasi pro-life position may be possible that is not, one that questions, for example, what kind of society would emerge where abortion became a substitute for birth control, education, the fight against poverty and disease and so on. The point here is simply that, in this case, there seems to be no risk to either position in listening more seriously to the other and recognizing its possible merit in widening our own interpretation of social meaning.

Americans may eventually come to agree with one another and with other societies as well over the issue of abortion. Indeed a technical solution may eventually be devised that satisfies all parties to the controversy. By recasting the debate as an interpretive one, however, we can already redirect our political energies away from our opponents' alleged sins against justice and morality; the different sides in the debate can begin to learn what is of value in the alternative interpretations of the meanings of the society's traditions and they can refine and develop their own. Even if by doing so we actually do come no closer to ending the debate, it seems to me that the public climate may be less hysterical and meanspirited. At the very least we will know what is at stake: not religious, moral or philosophical truth but mutual education and, indeed, ideally, a resolution to the debate consistent with the different ways we understand who we are as a society.

NOTES

Chapter 1 The Hermeneutic Turn in Recent Political Philosophy

1 See Jürgen Habermas, "Moralität und Sittlichkeit: Treffen Hegels Einwände gegen Kant auch auf die Diskursethik zu?" in *Moralität und Sittlichkeit*, ed. Wolfgang Kuhlmann (Suhrkamp, Frankfurt, 1986). In English as "Morality and Ethical Life: Does Hegel's Critique of Kant Apply to Discourse Ethics?" in *Moral Consciousness and Communicative Action*, trans. Christian Lenhardt and Shierry Weber Nicholsen (MIT Press, Cambridge, Mass., 1990).

2 John Rawls, *A Theory of Justice* (Harvard University Press, Cambridge, Mass., 1971).

3 Ibid., p. 11.

4 See Bruce Ackerman, *Social Justice in the Liberal State* (Yale University Press, New Haven, Conn., 1980), pp. 31ff.

5 See Michael Walzer, *Interpretation and Social Criticism* (Harvard University Press, Cambridge, Mass., 1987), pp. 14ff.

6 Bernard Williams, *Ethics and the Limits of Philosophy* (Harvard University Press, Cambridge, Mass., 1985), p. 140.

7 Ibid., p. 114.

8 Michael Walzer, *Spheres of Justice* (Basic Books, New York, 1983), p. 5.

9 See Hans-Georg Gadamer, *Truth and Method* (Seabury Press, New York, 1975), pp. 267ff.

10 See Charles Taylor, "Interpretation and the Sciences of Man," in *Philosophical Papers*, vol.2: *Philosophy and the Human Sciences* (Cambridge University Press, Cambridge, UK, 1985), p. 22.

11 Walzer, *Spheres of Justice*, p. xiv.

12 Richard Rorty, "Habermas and Lyotard on Postmodernity" in *Habermas and Modernity*, ed. Richard Bernstein (MIT Press, Cambridge, Mass., 1985), p. 166.

13 John Rawls, "Kantian Constructivism in Moral Theory", *Journal of Philosophy*, 76.9 (Summer, 1980), p. 519.
14 But see Walzer, *Interpretation and Social Criticism*, p. 8.
15 G. W. F. Hegel, The *Philosophy of Right* (1821), trans, T. M. Knox (Oxford University Press, Oxford, 1967), p. 11.
16 Ibid., p. 12.
17 Jürgen Habermas, "Die Kulturkritik der Neokonservativen in den USA und in der Bundesrepublik," in *Der Neue Unübersichtlichkeit* (Suhrkamp, Frankfurt, 1985), p. 41.
18 Michael Oakeshott, "On Being Conservative," in *Rationalism in Politics and Other Essays* (Basic Books, New York, 1962), p. 168.
19 In Peter Dews, ed. *Habermas: Autonomy and Solidarity: Interviews* (Verso, London, 1986), p. 207.
20 Richard Rorty, "Thugs and Theorists: A Reply to Bernstein," in *Political Theory*, 15.4, pp. 478ff.
21 Herbert Schnädelbach, "Was ist Neoaristotelismus?" in *Moralität und Sittlichkeit*, ed. Kuhlmann, p. 53.
22 Richard Rorty, "Pragmatism, Relativism, Irrationalism," in *Consequences of Pragmatism* (University of Minnesota Press, Minneapolis, 1982), p. 173.
23 Rawls, *A Theory of Justice*, p. 66.
24 Ibid., p. 83.

Chapter 2 Walzer and Social Interpretation

1 Michael Walzer, *Spheres of Justice* (Basic Books, New York, 1983), p. 8.
2 Ibid., p. 9.
3 Ibid., p. 313.
4 Ronald Dworkin, "To Each His Own," *New York Review of Books*, April 14, 1983, p. 6.
5 Walzer, *Spheres of Justice*, p. 75.
6 The vocabulary I am using here is that of Charles Taylor in "The Nature and Scope of Distributive Justice" in his *Philosophy and the Human Sciences*, vol. 2 of *Philosophical Papers* (Cambridge University Press, Cambridge, UK, 1985). It seems to me to articulate that which Walzer means with his remark: "Political community for the sake of provision, provision for the sake of community" (*Spheres of Justice*, p. 64).
7 *Spheres of Justice*, p. 89.
8 Ibid.
9 "To Each His Own," p. 4.
10 This is not to suggest that Dworkin actually adopts this atomistic approach in his own work. In fact, he quite explicitly argues against it (see *Law's Empire*, Harvard University Press, Cambridge, Mass., 1986, p. 63). Still, he seems often to rely upon it in order to criticize Walzer.
11 Charles Taylor, "Interpretation and the Sciences of Man," *Review of Metaphysics*, 25 (1971); reprinted in *Philosophy and the Human Sciences*, pp. 36–7.

12 Michael Walzer and Ronald Dworkin, "'Spheres of Justice': An Exchange," *New York Review of Books*, July 21, 1983, p. 45.

13 Ibid., p. 43.

14 Ibid.

15 "To Each His Own," p. 6.

16 "'Spheres of Justice': An Exchange," p. 43.

17 E. D. Hirsch, *Validity in Interpretation* (Yale University Press, New Haven, Conn., 1967), p. 31.

18 Ibid., p. 137.

19 R. G. Collingwood, *An Autobiography* (1939) (Oxford University Press, 1970), pp. 60ff.

20 See Martin Heidegger, *Being and Time* (1927), trans. J. Macquarrie and E. Robinson (Harper and Row, New York, 1962), p. H149.

21 See Joshua Cohen's review of *Spheres of Justice* in *Journal of Philosophy*, 83.8 (August, 1986), p. 464.

22 Taylor, "Interpretation and the Sciences of Man," p. 28.

23 *Spheres of Justice*, p. 314.

24 Ibid.

25 Richard Rorty, "Postmodernist Bourgeois Liberalism," in *Hermeneutics and Praxis* (University of Notre Dame, Notre Dame, Ind., 1985), p. 219.

26 *Spheres of Justice*, p. 298.

27 Ibid., p. 300.

28 See Karl Marx, *Capital*, vol. 1 (1867) (International Publishers, New York, 1974), ch. 6.

29 Quoted in Michael Walzer, *Interpretation and Social Criticism* (Harvard University Press, Cambridge, Mass., 1987), p. 42.

30 Walzer, *Interpretation and Social Criticism*, p. 44.

31 Ibid., p. 50.

Chapter 3   Rawls, Pluralism and Pragmatic Hermeneutics

1 John Rawls, "Kantian Constructivism in Moral Theory," *Journal of Philosophy*, 76.9 (Summer, 1980), p. 516.

2 Ibid., p. 518.

3 G. W. F. Hegel, *The Philosophy of Right* (1821), trans. T. M. Knox, (Oxford University Press, New York, 1967), p. 10.

4 "Kantian Constructivism," p. 518.

5 See also Richard Rorty, "The Priority of Democracy to Philosophy," in *The Virginia Statute for Religious Freedom*, ed. Merrill Peterson and Robert Vaughan (Cambridge University Press, Cambridge, UK, 1988), pp. 257–288.

6 John Rawls, "The Idea of an Overlapping Consensus" *Oxford Journal of Legal Studies*, 7.1, (1987), p. 5.

7 See "Kantian Constructivism," p. 517, and John Rawls, "Justice as Fairness: Political not Metaphysical," *Philosophy and Public Affairs*, 14 (Summer, 1985), p. 227.

8 "Justice as Fairness: Political not Metaphysical," p. 227. See also John

Rawls, "The Basic Liberties and their Priority," in *Liberty, Equality and Law*, ed. Sterling M. McMurrin (University of Utah Press, Salt Lake City, 1987), p. 14.

9   "Justice as Fairness: Political not Metaphysical," p. 229.

10   Ibid.

11   John Rawls, *A Theory of Justice*, (Harvard University Press, Cambridge, 1971), p. 261.

12   Ibid., p. 122.

13   Ibid., pp. 118–19.

14   Ibid., p. 120.

15   "Justice as Fairness: Political not Metaphysical," pp. 237–8.

16   "The Idea of an Overlapping Consensus," p. 9.

17   John Rawls, "The Priority of Right and Ideas of the Good," *Philosophy and Public Affairs*, 17 (Fall, 1988), pp. 265–6.

18   "The Idea of an Overlapping Consensus," p. 9.

19   Ibid., p. 13.

20   "Kantian Constructivism," p. 520.

21   See "The Priority of Right and Ideas of the Good," pp. 20–1.

22   Ibid.

23   "Kantian Constructivism," p. 517.

24   Ibid., p. 525.

25   Ibid., p. 532.

26   See Michael Sandel, *Liberalism and the Limits of Justice* (Cambridge University Press, Cambridge, UK, 1982).

27   "Kantian Constructivism," p. 545.

28   See also Amy Gutman, "Communitarian Critics of Liberalism," *Philosophy and Public Affairs*, 14.3, pp. 303–22.

29   "Kantian Constructivism," p. 544.

30   William Galston has a similar criticism of Rawls's account of moral persons, claiming that the highest-order interests Rawls finds essential to them would be necessarily contested by religious fundamentalists.

> But I wonder whether, for example, religious fundamentalists would regard the capacity to form and revise a conception of the good as a good at all, let alone a highest order interest of human beings. They might well declare that the best human life requires the capacity to receive an external good (God's truth) rather than to form a conception of the good for oneself, and to hold fast to that truth once received rather than to revise it. Rawls's Kantian conception would strike them as a sophisticated and therefore dangerous brand of secular humanism. Nor would they be impressed with the suggestion that whatever may be true of their nonpublic identity, their public personality should be understood in Rawls's fashion. From their perspective the disjunction between the public and nonpublic realms represents an injunction to set aside God's word, the only source of salvation, in determining the principles of our public order. I would argue, in short that Rawls's conception of moral personality will appeal only to those individuals who have accepted a particular understanding of the liberal political community and that our public culture is at present characterized not by consensus but, rather, by acute conflict over the adequacy of that understanding.

See Galston "Pluralism and Social Unity," *Ethics*, 99.4 (July, 1989), p. 714.

31 *A Theory of Justice*, p. 139.
32 "The Basic Liberties and their Priority," p. 5.
33 See *A Theory of Justice*, p. 83.
34 "The Basic Liberties and their Priority," pp. 42–3.
35 Ibid., p. 45.
36 "The Idea of an Overlapping Consensus," p. 8.
37 *A Theory of Justice*, p. 216.
38 Ibid.
39 "The Idea of an Overlapping Consensus," p. 7.

Chapter 4   Legal Interpretation and Constraint

1 For a more sophisticated statement of this position see Roberto M. Unger, *The Critical Legal Studies Movement* (Harvard University Press, Cambridge, Mass., 1983).
2 Owen Fiss, "Objectivity and Interpretation," *Stanford Law Review* 34, (April, 1982), p. 746.
3 Ronald Dworkin, "How Law is like Literature" in *A Matter of Principle* (Harvard University Press, Cambridge, Mass., 1985), p. 163.
4 See Dworkin's view of the applicative moment of interpretation in Ronald Dworkin, *Law's Empire* (Harvard University Press, Cambridge, Mass., 1986), pp. 55–6.
5 *Law's Empire*, p. 52.
6 "How Law is like Literature," p. 149.
7 Ibid., p. 233.
8 Ibid., p.153.
9 Ronald Dworkin, "On Interpretation and Objectivity," in *A Matter of Principle*, pp. 169–70.
10 "How Law is like Literature," p. 150–1.
11 *Law's Empire*, p. 219.
12 Ibid., p. 178.
13 Ibid., p. 182.
14 Ibid., p. 184.
15 Ibid., p. 240.
16 Ibid., p. 241.
17 Ibid., p. 242.
18 Ibid., pp. 248–9.
19 Ibid., p. 405.
20 Ibid., p. 240.
21 Ibid., p. 241.
22 Ibid., p. 380.
23 Ibid., p. 388.
24 *Plessy v. Ferguson* 163 U.S. 537 (1896).
25 Ibid.
26 Charles Tayler, "Interpretation and the Sciences of Man," in *Philosophical*

Papers, vol. 2: *Philosophy and the Human Sciences* (Cambridge University Press, Cambridge, UK, 1985), p. 54.

27 *Law's Empire*, p. 256.
28 "How Law is like Literature," pp. 164–5.
29 "Objectivity and Interpretation," p. 744.
30 Ibid., p. 745
31 Ibid.
32 Ibid., p. 748.
33 See Stanley Fish, "Fish v. Fiss," in *Stanford Law Review*, 36 (July, 1984), p. 1342.
34 Ibid., p. 1331.
35 See Owen Fiss, "Conventionalism," *Southern California Law Review*, 58, (1985), p. 197.

Chapter 5   Habermas and the Conflict of Interpretations

1 Jürgen Habermas, *The Theory of Communicative Action*, vol. 1: *Reason and the Rationalization of Society* (Beacon Press, Boston, 1984), p. 286.
2 Jürgen Habermas, "Diskursethik: Notizen zu einem Begründungsprogramm," in *Moralbewusstsein und Kommunicatives Handeln* (Suhrkamp, Frankfurt, 1983), p. 68. In English as "Discourse Ethics: Notes on a Program of Philosophical Justification," in *Moral Consciousness and Communicative Action*, trans. Christian Lenhardt and Shierry Weber Nicholsen (MIT Press, Cambridge, Mass., 1990), p. 58.
3 *The Theory of Communicative Action*, vol. 1, p. 288.
4 See Jürgen Habermas, "Handlungen, Sprechakte, Sprachlict vermittelte Interaktionen und Lebenswelt," in *Nachmetaphysiches Denken* (Suhrkamp, Frankfurt, 1988), p. 71–2.
5 *The Theory of Communication Action*, vol. 1, p. 24.
6 Jürgen Habermas, "Justice and Solidarity: On the Discussion Concerning 'Stage 6,'" in *The Moral Domain: Essays on the Ongoing Discussion, between Philosophy and the Social Sciences*, ed. Thomas E. Wren (MIT Press, Cambridge, Mass., 1990), p. 235.
7 Jürgen Habermas, "Moralität und Sittlichkeit: Treffen Hegels Einwände gegen Kant auch auf die Diskursethik zu?" in *Moralität und Sittlichkeit*, ed. Wolfgang Kuhlmann (Suhrkamp, Frankfurt, 1986), p. 18. In English as "Morality and Ethical Life: Does Hegel's Critique of Kant Apply to Discourse Ethics?" in *Moral Consciousness and Communicative Action*, see p. 197.
8 "Diskursethik," p. 97 ("Discourse Ethics," p. 157).
9 "Moralität und Sittlichkeit," p. 18 ("Morality and Ethical Life," see p. 197).
10 John Rawls, *A Theory of Justice* (Harvard University Press, Cambridge, Mass., 1971), p. 140.
11 T. M. Scanlon, "Contractualism and Utilitarianism," in *Utilitarianism and Beyond*, ed. Amartya Sen and Bernard Williams (Cambridge University Press, New York, 1982), p. 113.

12 Ibid., p. 116.

13 Ibid., p. 122.

14 Ibid.

15 Thomas McCarthy, *The Critical Theory of Jürgen Habermas* (MIT Press, Cambridge, Mass., 1978), p. 326.

16 "Justice and Solidarity," pp. 235–6.

17 See Ronald Dworkin, "Justice and Rights," in Dworkin, *Taking Rights Seriously* (Harvard University Press, Cambridge, Mass., 1977), pp. 150–83.

18 "Diskursethik" p. 96 ("Discourse Ethics," see p. 86).

19 "Moralität und Sittlichkeit," p. 25 ("Morality and Ethical Life," see p. 209).

20 See, for example, Norman Daniels, "Equal Liberty and Unequal Worth of Liberty" in *Reading Rawls* ed. Daniels (Basic Books, New York, 1976), pp. 253–81.

21 "Moralität und Sittlichkeit," p. 16 ("Morality and Ethical Life," see p. 195).

22 The idea for this example comes from Seyla Benhabib's "In the Shadow of Aristotle and Hegel: Communicative Ethics and Current Controversies in Practical Philosophy" *Philosophical Forum*, 21.1–2, (Fall–Winter, 1989–90), p. 10. She uses it to show the relative weakness of U as compared to Kant's categorical imperative, a weakness she attributes to Habermas's overly consequentialist formulation since "the least that a universalist ethical theory ought to do is to cover the same ground as what Kant had described as negative duties." Although Habermas has two answers to this objection, both raise what I shall be viewing as interpretive problems.

23 Hannah Arendt, "Reflections on Little Rock," *Dissent*, 6.1 (Winter, 1959), pp. 45–56.

24 "Moralität und Sittlichkeit," p. 26 ("Morality and Ethical Life," p. 205).

25 Ibid.

26 "Diskursethik," p. 102 ("Discourse Ethics," see p. 92).

27 "Moralität und Sittlichkeit," p. 25 ("Morality and Ethical Life," p. 204).

28 *The Theory of Communicative Action*, vol. 1, p. 20.

29 Ibid.

30 Ibid.

31 Ibid., p. 41.

32 See Jürgen Habermas, *Knowledge and Human Interests*, trans. Jeremy Shapiro (Beacon Press, Boston, 1971), chs 10–12, and "The Hermeneutic Claim to Universality," in *Contemporary Hermeneutics*, ed. Josef Bleicher (Routledge and Kegan Paul, London, 1980). I shall be discussing therapeutic critique again in chapter 7.

33 "Moralität und Sittlichkeit," pp. 25–6 ("Morality and Ethical Life," p. 205).

34 See Habermas, "Justice and Solidarity," pp. 248–9.

35 "Moralität und Sittlichkeit," pp. 27–8 ("Morality and Ethical Life," p. 207).

36 See Hans-Georg Gadamer, *Truth and Method* (Seabury Press, New York,

1975), pp. 274–305.

37 *The Theory of Communicative Action*, vol. 1, p. 17.
38 "Justice and Solidarity," p. 247.
39 Jürgen Habermas, *Legitimation Crisis*, trans. Thomas McCarthy (Beacon Press, Boston, 1975), pp. 108–9 (emphases in text).
40 "Diskursethik," p. 76 ("Discourse Ethics," p. 66), (emphasis mine).
41 See ibid., p. 113 (p. 104).
42 Ibid., p. 78 (pp. 67–8).
43 Jürgen Habermas, "Questions and Counterquestions," trans. James Bohman, in *Habermas and Modernity*, ed. Richard Bernstein (MIT Press, Cambridge, Mass., 1985), p. 203. See also "Modernity versus Post-modernity," trans. Seyla Benhabib, *New German Critique*, 22 (1981).
44 "Questions and Counterquestions," p. 202. See also David Ingram, *Habermas and the Dialectic of Reason* (Yale University Press, New Haven, Conn., 1986).

Chapter 6 Dealing with Interpretive Conflict

1 John Rawls, "The Idea of an Overlapping Consensus," *Oxford Journal of Legal Studies*, 7.1 (19870, p. 7.
2 Charles Taylor "The Nature and Scope of Distributive Justice," in *Philosophical Papers*, vol. 2: *Philosophy and the Human Sciences* (Cambridge University Press, Cambridge, UK, 1985).
3 Ibid., p. 292.
4 Ibid., p. 305.
5 Robert Nozick, *Anarchy, State and Utopia* (Basic Books, New York, 1974).
6 Taylor, "The Nature and Scope of Distributive Justice," p. 307.
7 Ibid., p. 311.
8 See John Rawls, *A Theory of Justice* (Harvard University Press, Cambridge, Mass., 1971), pp. 103–4
9 Taylor, "The Nature and Scope of Distributive Justice," p. 315.
10 Ibid., p. 310.
11 Ibid., p. 313.
12 Richard Rorty, "Postmodernist Bourgeois Liberalism," in *Hermeneutics and Praxis* (University of Notre Dame, Notre Dame, Ind., 1985), p. 219.
13 Alasdair MacIntyre, *Whose Justice? Which Rationality?* (University of Notre Dame Press, Notre Dame, Ind., 1988), p. 12.
14 Ibid., p. 354.
15 Ibid., p. 326.
16 Ibid., p. 12.
17 Ibid., p. 358.
18 Ibid., pp. 361–5.
19 Ibid., p. 361.
20 Ibid., p. 378.
21 Ibid., p. 382.
22 Hence, MacIntyre rejects the claim associated with Donald Davidson

that a complete commensurability between languages is necessary to the elementary task of identifying the speakers of an alien language as having a language and indeed a mind at all. (See Donald Davidson, "On the Very Idea of a Conceptual Scheme" in *Post-Analytic Philosophy*, ed. John Rajehman and Cornel West Columbia University Press, New York, 1985), pp. 129–44.) MacIntyre admits that there must "always be something in common between any two languages or any two sets of thoughts" (*Whose Justice? Which Rationality?*, p. 371). The possession of two first languages, however, seems to remain the means, for him, by which two languages can be brought into relation to one another in such a way that their distinctiveness and hence the possibility of their challenging one another are preserved.

23 *Whose Justice? Which Rationality?*, p. 388.
24 Ibid., p. 7.
25 Ibid., p. 336.
26 Cited from Rawls, *A Theory of Justice* p. 554, in MacIntyre, *Whose Justice? Which Rationality?*, p. 337.
27 *Whose Justice? Which Rationality?*, p. 342 (emphasis in text).
28 Ibid., p. 343.
29 Ibid., p. 344.
30 Ibid., p. 344.

Chapter 7   Hermeneutic Conversation and the Critique of Ideology

1 John Stuart Mill, *On Liberty* (1859) (Bobbs-Merrill, Indianopolis, 1975), p. 21.
2 Ibid., pp. 24–5
3 Ibid., pp. 43–4.
4 Ibid., p. 53.
5 Ibid., pp. 53–5.
6 Ibid., p. 21.
7 Jürgen Habermas, "The Hermeneutic Claim to Universality," in *Contemporary Hermeneutics*, ed. Josef Bleicher (Routledge and Kegan Paul, London, 1980), p. 191.
8 "Moralität und Sittlichkeit: Treffen Hegels Einwände gegen Kant auch auf die Diskursethik zu?" in *Moralität und Sittlichkeit*, ed. Wolfgang Kuhlmann (Suhrkamp, Frankfurt, 1986), p. 26. In English as "Morality and Ethical Life: Does Hegel's Critique of Kant Apply to Discourse Ethics?" in *Moral Consciousness and Communicative Action*, trans. Christian Lenhardt and Shierry Weber Nicholsen (MIT Press, Cambridge, Mass., 1990), p. 205.
9 See, for example, Charles Taylor, "Interpretation and the Sciences of Man," in *Philosophical Papers*, vol. 2: *Philosophy and the Human Sciences* (Cambridge University Press, Cambridge, UK, 1985), pp. 15–58, and Peter Winch, "Understanding a Primitive Society," in *Understanding and Social Inquiry*, ed. Fred Dallmayr and Thomas McCarthy (University of Notre Dame Press, Notre Dame, Ind., 1977).

10 Habermas, "The Hermeneutic Claim to Universality," in *Contemporary Hermeneutics*, p. 194.

11 Jürgen Habermas, *On the Logic of the Social Sciences*, trans. Shierry Weber Nicholsen and Jerry A. Stark (Polity Press, Cambridge, UK, and MIT Press, Cambridge, Mass., 1988), p. 187.

12 Jürgen Habsermas, "What is Universal Pragmatics," in *Communication and the Evolution of Society* ((Heinemann Educational, London, 1979), p. 11.

13 Ibid., p. 12.

14 Ibid., p. 14.

15 Jürgen Habermas, "Reconstruction and Interpretation in the Social Sciences," in *Moral Consciousness and Communicative Action*, trans. Christian Lenhardt and Shierry Weber Nicholsen (Polity Press, Cambridge, UK and MIT Press, Cambridge, Mass., 1990), p. 31.

16 Ibid.

17 "What is Universal Pragmatics," p. 16.

18 "Reconstruction and Interpretation in the Social Sciences," p. 32.

19 Michael Walzer, *Interpretation and Social Criticism* (Harvard University Press, Cambridge, Mass., 1987), p. 44.

20 In Nancy Fraser, *Unruly Practices: Power, Discourse and Gender in Contemporary Social Theory* (Polity Press, Cambridge, UK and University of Minnesota Press, Minneapolis, 1989), pp. 161–87.

21 Ibid., p. 164.

22 Ibid., p. 165.

23 Ibid., p. 166.

24 Ibid.

25 Ibid., p. 175.

26 Ibid., p. 166.

27 Ibid., p. 181.

28 Ibid., p. 182.

29 Ibid., pp. 181–2.

30 Habermas, "The Hermeneutic Claim to Universality," p. 205.

31 Richard Rorty, "Habermas and Lyotard on Postmodernity," in *Habermas and Modernity*, ed. Richard Bernstein (MIT Press, Cambridge, Mass., 1985), p. 164.

32 Richard Rorty, "Pragmatism, Relativism, Irrationalism," in *Consequences of Pragmatism* (University of Minnesota Press, Minneapolis, 1982), p. 173.

33 Nancy Fraser, "Struggle over Needs: Outline of a Socialist-Feminist Critical Theory of Late Capitalist Political Culture," in *Unruly Practices*, p. 187.

Chapter 8   Conclusion

1 Michael Walzer, *Spheres of Justice*, (Basic Books, New York, 1983), p. 313.

INDEX

Studies in Contemporary German Social Thought
Thomas McCarthy, General Editor

Theodor W. Adorno, *Against Epistemology: A Metacritique*

Theodor W. Adorno, *Hegel: Three Studies*

Theodor W. Adorno, *Prisms*

Karl-Otto Apel, *Understanding and Explanation: A Transcendental-Pragmatic Perspective*

Seyla Benhabib and Fred Dallmayr, editors, *The Communicative Ethics Controversy*

Richard J. Bernstein, editor, *Habermas and Modernity*

Ernst Bloch, *Natural Law and Human Dignity*

Ernst Bloch, *The Principle of Hope*

Ernst Bloch, *The Utopian Function of Art and Literature: Selected Essays*

Hans Blumenberg, *The Genesis of the Copernican World*

Hans Blumenberg, *The Legitimacy of the Modern Age*

Hans Blumenberg, *Work on Myth*

Susan Buck-Morss, *The Dialectics of Seeing: Walter Benjamin and the* Arcades Project

Craig Calhoun, editor, *Habermas and the Public Sphere*

Jean Cohen and Andrew Arato, *Civil Society and Political Theory*

Helmut Dubiel, *Theory and Politics: Studies in the Development of Critical Theory*

John Forester, editor, *Critical Theory and Public Life*

David Frisby, *Fragments of Modernity: Theories of Modernity in the Work of Simmel, Kracauer and Benjamin*

Hans-Georg Gadamer, *Philosophical Apprenticeships*

Hans-Georg Gadamer, *Reason in the Age of Science*

Jürgen Habermas, *Justification and Application: Remarks on Discourse Ethics*

Jürgen Habermas, *On the Logic of the Social Sciences*

Jürgen Habermas, *Moral Consciousness and Communicative Action*

Jürgen Habermas, *The New Conservatism: Cultural Criticism and the Historians' Debate*

Jürgen Habermas, *The Philosophical Discourse of Modernity: Twelve Lectures*

Jürgen Habermas, *Philosophical-Political Profiles*

Jürgen Habermas, *Postmetaphysical Thinking: Philosophical Essays*

Jürgen Habermas, *The Structural Transformation of the Public Sphere: An Inquiry into a Category of Bourgeois Society*

Jürgen Habermas, editor, *Observations on "The Spiritual Situation of the Age"*

Axel Honneth, *The Critique of Power: Reflective Stages in a Critical Social Theory*

Axel Honneth and Hans Joas, editors, *Communicative Action: Essays on Jürgen Habermas's* The Theory of Communicative Action

Axel Honneth, Thomas McCarthy, Claus Offe, and Albrecht Wellmer, editors, *Cultural-Political Interventions in the Unfinished Project of Enlightenment*

Axel Honneth, Thomas McCarthy, Claus Offe, and Albrecht Wellmer, editors, *Philosophical Interventions in the Unfinished Project of Enlightenment*

Max Horkheimer, *Between Philosophy and Social Science: Selected Early Writings*

Hans Joas, *G. H. Mead: A Contemporary Re-examination of His Thought*

Reinhart Koselleck, *Critique and Crisis: Enlightenment and the Pathogenesis of Modern Society*

Reinhart Koselleck, *Futures Past: On the Semantics of Historical Time*

Harry Liebersohn, *Fate and Utopia in German Sociology, 1887-1923*

Herbert Marcuse, *Hegel's Ontology and the Theory of Historicity*

Gil G. Noam and Thomas Wren, editors, *The Moral Self: Building a Better Paradigm*

Guy Oakes, *Weber and Rickert: Concept Formation in the Cultural Sciences*

Claus Offe, *Contradictions of the Welfare State*

Claus Offe, *Disorganized Capitalism: Contemporary Transformations of Work and Politics*

Helmut Peukert, *Science, Action, and Fundamental Theology: Toward a Theology of Communicative Action*

Joachim Ritter, *Hegel and the French Revolution: Essays on the* Philosophy of Right

Alfred Schmidt, *History and Structure: An Essay on Hegelian-Marxist and Structuralist Theories of History*

Dennis Schmidt, *The Ubiquity of the Finite: Hegel, Heidegger, and the Entitlements of Philosophy*

Carl Schmitt, *The Crisis of Parliamentary Democracy*

Carl Schmitt, *Political Romanticism*

Carl Schmitt, *Political Theology: Four Chapters on the Concept of Sovereignty*

Gary Smith, editor, *On Walter Benjamin: Critical Essays and Recollections*

Michael Theunissen, *The Other: Studies in the Social Ontology of Husserl, Heidegger, Sartre, and Buber*

Ernst Tugendhat, *Self-Consciousness and Self-Determination*

Georgia Warnke, *Justice and Interpretation*

Mark Warren, *Nietzsche and Political Thought*

Albrecht Wellmer, *The Persistence of Modernity: Essays on Aesthetics, Ethics and Postmodernism*

Thomas E. Wren, editor, *The Moral Domain: Essays in the Ongoing Discussion between Philosophy and the Social Sciences*

Lambert Zuidervaart, *Adorno's Aesthetic Theory: The Redemption of Illusion*